KATHARINE STEWART lives in Inverness. Born in 1914, she spent her early years in Musselburgh, and studied French at Edinburgh University. Then, during the war years, she worked for the Admiralty in London. She then moved to Abriachan, near Inverness, where she ran a croft and wrote documentaries for the BBC.

She has written numerous articles for various magazines, as well as several books. She was instrumental in setting up the museum at Abriachan. In April 2005 she received the Saltire Society Highland Branch Award for Contribution to the Understanding of Highland Culture, in recognition of her many works.

D1458170

Cattle on a Thousand Hills

Farming culture in the Highlands of Scotland

KATHARINE STEWART

Luath Press Limited

EDINBURGH

www.luath.co.uk

This book is for my family.
They were with me all the way.

First published 2010
Reprinted 2011

ISBN: 978-1-906817-44-2

The paper used in this book is recyclable. It is made from
low chlorine pulps produced in a low energy, low emissions manner
from renewable forests.

Printed and bound by
Bell & Bain Ltd., Glasgow

Typeset in 11 point Sabon
by 3btype.com

Contents

Acknowledgements

I HAVE MANY PEOPLE to thank for help in the writing of this book – Janey Clarke of the Highland Livestock Heritage Society, Alistair Macleod, the Highland Council genealogist and Anne Fraser, assistant genealogist, the staff of the Inverness Library reference and lending departments, and Una Cochrane, the writer on Highland cattle.

I would also like to thank my daughter Hilda, grandson Mark and son-in-law Jack Hesling. I should like to thank Leila Cruickshank and my editor Rob Fletcher for their help in putting the book together.

Special thanks go to Roy Dennis who wrote the foreword and contributed the photographs on pages 69, 78, 105 and 113.

Special thanks, also, to Jim Reid, grandson of Charles Reid, who kindly allowed his grandfather's photograph of cattle in the hills to be featured on the cover of the book and for other phototgraphs on pages 101 and 102.

Foreword

KATHARINE STEWART'S NEW BOOK reminds us of our ancestry and heritage – a farming culture based on thousands of years of close partnership with cattle. She brings to the reader not only the pure pleasure of keeping cows, but also the friendships they create and the roles that the animals play in our history and culture. She also brings to mind remarkable images of the first Bronze Age travellers, who arrived in Britain with their hardy Celtic breeds, pushing aside the native aurochs as they sought grazing for their own domestic beasts. And thus started, as Katharine reveals, at least 5,000 years of a cattle society – a civilisation based around milk, butter, cheese, blood, meat, hide and bone.

Cattle are still in my blood, as they are in Katharine's. I'm not very keen on sheep and goats and I'm rather shy of horses, but cows I enjoy. Although I've never regularly milked, I have felt the closeness of leaning against a flank and hearing the warm milk hit the bucket. I've also felt that pride of moving cattle from winter to summer grazings and back – the skittishness of cows heading for the hills with tiny calves, and the 'holier than thou' feeling of holding up tourist traffic on a narrow road. It is a way of reaching back to our roots and reordering the importance of the day.

My own life has been spent in nature conservation, a daily involvement with research and management of rare birds in the Highlands and Islands. In my earlier years, it occasionally involved travelling to a small loch above Loch Ness, close to Katharine's old croft, where beautiful Slavonian grebes used to breed, and the book takes me back to those days.

It also reminds me of my lifelong desire to see ecosystems restored and functioning properly, and the wish to see the white-tailed eagle, red kite, beaver and lynx back where they belong. Sadly one mammal, the aurochs, cannot be restored, having been exterminated by Man. Thankfully, however, most of its genes and much of its behaviour have been saved in our domestic cattle. And traditional breeds farmed by traditional means can carry out most of the ecological roles in the countryside that their lost ancestors once performed.

The animals are essential for the ecology of our countryside and have a pivotal place in nature conservation. Yet, unfortunately, the numbers of cattle kept in this way have declined dramatically and continue to do so – courtesy of increased bureaucracy, keeping small numbers of cattle is now mind-blowingly difficult.

Yet there is a desperate need for more traditional breeds to be grazed on nature's best lands, in order to help restore and manage these ecosystems for the benefit of all fauna and flora. At the same time it should be made easier and more profitable to keep them, and we should try to restore cattle to their rightful place in society – as Katharine illustrates in this beautiful book.

Roy Dennis MBE

Preface
Cattle on the Croft

SOME FIFTY YEARS AGO my husband and I came from Edinburgh to work a croft in Caiplich, Abriachan, a small settlement 800 feet up in the hills to the north of Loch Ness.

My husband's forebears were crofters in Perthshire and I had farming ancestors in Galloway, so agriculture must have been in the blood. Before we moved north we had grown food in a small way, had kept poultry and bees and had escaped to the hills whenever we could.

In Caiplich we found ourselves in a community of crofters, native to the area, who all spoke Gaelic as well as English, and worked their crofts in the traditional way. They made us, and our small daughter, unreservedly welcome.

We soon acquired a small herd of black Aberdeen Angus cattle, then three score blackface sheep, numerous poultry and Charlie – a garron or working pony, who soon became one of the family! We also had a tractor, one of the few in the immediate vicinity.

After a while we became competent enough to take part in the usual community activities of clipping and dipping the sheep, of harvesting, of herding cattle and so on.

Our daughter, Hilda, like all croft children, also joined in happily – feeding motherless lambs from a bottle and dumping sheaves of corn into stooks. Later she would gaze in amazement as the travelling threshing-mill arrived and began to turn the sheaves into grain and straw.

We followed the usual five-year rotation of crops – oats, grass for hay, potatoes, turnips, then fallow. The oats were harvested with the binder and made into stacks, which was a communal job. Making hay was another community activity, although we sometimes had to hang it on the fences to dry before stacking! The potatoes and turnips were stored in clamps – long shallow pits covered with straw or rushes to keep out the frost.

On winter evenings we enjoyed many a ceilidh, a gathering in someone's house, for the exchange of news and gossip and perhaps a tune on the 'box', as the accordion was known, and a song or two. Our neighbours would tell us about people and happenings of older times, their powers of recall amazing us.

They told us of one neighbour known as 'The Drover', droving being in his blood. The days of the long droves to the south were over, of course, but he still liked to take cattle on the hoof, even the ten miles to the market in Inverness. He would collect twenty or thirty beasts from the area, two or three boys would have a couple of days off school to deal with the herding, and off they would go. A stop overnight in a friendly farmer's field and they would be fit and fresh for the market early next morning.

One day, it seems, they were too fresh. In spite of frantic herding by the boys, when passing down the High Street of

Part of our small herd grazing the rough ground

Inverness a frisky bullock crashed into, of all places, a dairy! Not too much damage was done, compensation was arranged for later, and the drove moved on. That story made the headlines in the local press.

When we asked why a small island in the burn which ran through our croft was called the 'island of cheeses' we were told that cheese made up in a shieling on the hill to the west had by mischance landed in the water and been carried downstream before being washed up on the island. It was still edible, despite its perilous journey!

These tales and others, told with all the verve and accuracy of the born story-teller, brought the past vividly before us.

Along with four other crofters we had the right, on a

nearby hill, to 'graze sheep, cut peats and bleach linen.' This last must have dated from the time when flax was grown to make linen thread. As a result we had room for the sheep. They mostly looked after themselves – lambing on their own, and being fed a little hay only in the worst of the winter weather. Hilda loved the lambs, of course, but the sheep as a whole did not inspire the affection we felt for the cattle, or for our hard-working garron.

My husband went away from time to time, as was the custom among crofters, to work at something that would bring in a little cash. During these periods my daughter and I managed the croft on our own.

We always hoped that no disaster would occur during these times. As we were quite far off any beaten track we sometimes had to act as amateur vets in an emergency. 'Bloat' for instance, a swelling of the stomach caused by over-indulgence in sweet, spring grass, had to be dealt with promptly by piercing the organ to allow the gas to escape. Calving could be tricky but, luckily, we had no problems with it, only strength and common sense being needed in a difficult birth.

There were two bulls within walking distance to which our cows could go at the appropriate time. Artificial insemination was not commonly resorted to in our day. We were lucky not to have foot-and-mouth around and to be farming before the time of BSE and blue tongue. The cattle were, however, regularly tested for brucellosis and TB.

We kept one cow to provide milk for the house, the

others allowed their calves to suckle. We had many names for the cows, of course, many of which were slightly daft – May, who always calved in May, Caroline, who resembled an old friend of mine, and so on. The female calves, as they grew on as heifers, acquired names too. We didn't name the boys – even though we had seen them grow from lively, dancing creatures, cavorting about on their little spindly legs, into the castrated, burly beasts known as bullocks – because we knew they would eventually be destined for market. But we loved them, too, and hoped that when they went to market they would reach a dealer who had a flowery meadow for them to enjoy before they met their final fate.

With a small herd such as ours we could get to know each beast individually. We knew Queenie, for example, would always be the first at the byre door on a cold winter evening, May would be the one bellowing to get out on a fine morning. Just as we knew them and enjoyed their company I'm sure they enjoyed ours.

My closest contact with any of the herd was with the cow I milked for the house. We called her Hope and she gave us many well-doing calves over the years. She was a cross-bred shorthorn, sturdy, with a reddish-brown silky coat. As I leaned towards her flank while milking I could feel the life-beat pulsing in her.

I sang to her, of course, although – sadly – not in Gaelic. Her favourite song was 'Lily Marlene'. If I sang anything different she would turn her head and give me a look from her big dark eyes.

One cold spring morning I had a lovely surprise. As the first drops of milk spurted into the pail a blackbird, who had taken up residence in the byre over the winter, began to sing his little inward song, in rehearsal for the full-throated version he would sing from the branch of the rowan later on. This was a moment of delight which will be with me always.

CHAPTER ONE

The Early Cattle

ABOUT 10,000 YEARS AGO, when the ice was retreating, allowing vegetation to push through, aurochs were making their way across the land mass which is now the North Sea, to Britain.

Originating either in North India or Central Asia, this wild ox, the *Bos primigenius taurus*, had spread to North Africa and into Europe, a huge powerful beast, standing six feet at the shoulder and weighing several tons. The bull was dark reddish brown, with a line of paler hair down the back. The long horns, white and black-tipped, curved out and forward, and then up. The cows were smaller and paler in colour, the matriarchs of the herd. Cave paintings in France, dating from about 15,000 BC, show cattle of this type.

Some 5,000 years ago a slow process of domestication of the aurochs began to take place in Britain. The skull of an aurochs from about this time can be seen in the Falconer Museum in Forres, a small town in north-east Scotland. It was unearthed on East Grange

Early cattle painted on cave wall

Early cattle. Dordogne, France

farm in Morayshire when drains were being dug in 1898 and was acquired by the museum after being checked by an expert from Edinburgh. It is in remarkably good condition.

In 2007 two separate horns were found fifteen feet below the surface in the same area. They are also thought to be from aurochs. Traces of these animals – bones and carcasses – have been found as far north as Caithness.

It must have taken courage and skill of an unimaginable kind to bring an aurochs down with the weapons and implements available at the time, let alone to tame one. Sometimes we underestimate the power of these early people. Is it possible that a young beast could have wandered near a human settlement, near enough to be manhandled and enclosed?

However it happened, this domestication was of enormous significance, as it led to the progress towards developed farming, which was in turn the basis of European and Asiatic culture.

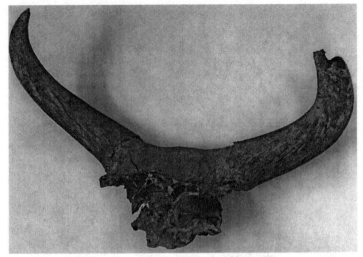

Skull of Aurochs
Falconer Museum, Forres

It is thought that the last of the aurochs – a small herd in a remote part of Poland – were shot for sport in 1657. In the 1920s, however, two Austrian scientists, brothers Heinz and Lutz Heck, tried to recreate the aurochs by crossing Spanish and French fighting cattle with other breeds, including Highland cattle. About 150 animals resulted, the bulls black, the cows reddish brown. They appeared in zoos in Munich and Berlin.

The breeding of these cattle was part of Hitler's obsession with all things Aryan and original, and was mirrored by his search for the roots of the Germanic people themselves.

Heck cattle at Edinburgh Zoo
© RZSS

After the Second World War most of the animals were destroyed, but some survived and, in April 2009, a small herd of these Heck cattle – bulls, cows and calves – was acquired by Edinburgh zoo.

About the time of the initial domestication of the aurochs, Celtic immigrant people were bringing their shorthorn cattle to parts of Britain, travelling precariously in small boats known as curraghs. These beasts were the forebears of the small black cattle of the Western Isles of Scotland. They were to become known as 'kyloes' from the way they swum or were ferried across the kyles, or sea-inlets, to the mainland. They became longer-haired, due to climatic conditions, and reddish-brown in colour. A touch of the aurochs? Who knows what couplings may have taken place? This colour was favoured, particularly in later times, when much of the black was bred out. Today, of course, they have become Highland cattle – the picture postcard breed so beloved by tourists in Scotland.

These beasts were descendants – as were all cattle – of the aurochs which had roamed in the Celtic dominated parts of Europe. In the early centuries AD, the

Cattle on a drove, Kyle 1888

Roman and the Saxon invaders were to bring in different breeds of cattle, mainly to the south of Britain. Later on the Norse, in the ninth century, brought in red or dun polled cattle to the Highlands, which would readily have acclimatised. Other breeds suited to the north, such as the Aberdeen Angus cross, did not appear until the nineteenth century. In the twentieth century some Herefords were introduced experimentally. In the conditions of the north all beasts had to be hardy to survive.

To return to the early immigrants, the Romans and others were to bring in other types of cattle, so diversification went on. Whatever their size and disposition these animals – both bulls and cows – were creatures of consequence. Myths and legends concerning them are many.

As an epitome of strength and virility, with his massive head and shoulders, the bull became a totem animal of the early peoples in many parts of the world; and the cow, with her bountiful source of life-giving milk, was equally valued. To this day, in India, the cow is venerated. It is said that she saved the life of the Hindu god Krishna by giving him milk when he was starving. Anyone harming a cow today is severely punished. In the Mediterranean area the bull has been revered in many places, while in Egypt pilgrims came to worship and admire the sacred bull Apis in the temple of Memphis.

Minos, the legendary ruler of Crete, about 5,000 years ago, gave his name to the Minotaur, the fabulous monster of legend, which had the body of a man and the head of a bull. A ritual of bull-leaping would take place on the island as part of a magical or religious cult. Bull-fighting in Spain and southern France is most probably a legacy of the Romans. Today the bulls still run through the streets of Pamplona in Spain, the crowds goading them to their own peril.

In early Ireland, Maeb, Queen of Connacht, invaded Ulster to take possession of a famed brown bull in the legendary battle known as the 'Cattle Raid of Cooley'. The bull was famed for his prowess as a progenitor of good stock and was sent into Connacht for his own safety. The white-horned bull of Connacht heard the brown fellow bellowing, however, and in the resulting battle the brown bull killed the white before dying himself, in a story that illustrates the conflict between Ulster and Connacht.

In Burghead, on the coast of Morayshire, a number of granite slabs with deeply incised bulls carved on them were dredged up from the harbour in the late 1800s. Could they have been part of a ritual to placate the sea gods in their fury? They were clearly associated with the nearby Pictish fort. Not far from Burghead, at Portmahomack, where a Pictish settlement has been discovered, a stone head was found bearing the charming image of a cow licking her calf. This stone may be seen in the museum of the Tarbat Historic Trust in the old church at Portmahomack.

Carvings such as these demonstrate how cattle must have been very much a part of everyday life in those early times. There were still plenty of their wild cousins about too, providing sport for the chiefs as deer do in the Highlands

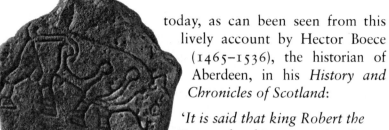

Symbol stone with a figure of a bull deeply incised; one of several found at Burghead, Morayshire. Pictish 6th–7th century AD

today, as can been seen from this lively account by Hector Boece (1465–1536), the historian of Aberdeen, in his *History and Chronicles of Scotland*:

'*It is said that king Robert the Bruce after his coronation [in 1310] went to ane hunting in the wood of Caledon... he escapit narrowly with his life for ane of the bullis, eftir that he was sair woundit be the huntaris, rushit feirslie on the King howbeit he had na wapanis in his hand to debait himself fra the dent thereof...one man of greit spreit quhilk was standing neirby lap afore the king and most allaneilie kest the bull be manifest forced to the erd bot held him quhill the remanent huntaris slew him with thair wapannis. This man, that rescursit the king was callit Turnbull, and was rewardit with rich lands be the king.*'

This bull would have been one of the wild white cattle found in 'Caledon' – a large area of central Scotland. They were probably descended from those brought in by the Romans. The Druids certainly revered them, for white cattle were considered worthy of sacrifice. The pale creatures were eventually enclosed in parkland and their descendants are now at Chillingham in Northumberland and at Cadzow

Park in Lanarkshire. They retain their wild nature and will not readily tolerate human contact to this day.

In 1851 Sam Bough, the artist, had discovered the white cattle in Cadzow forest, as had Horatio McCullogh. Bough would chase the cattle, which would then run off for a short distance before turning and rushing at the intruder. Wisely, Bough climbed into a tree to watch and record his subjects.

Sir Walter Scott, in 1802, wrote the 'Ballad of Cadzow Castle,' in which he says:

> *Mightiest of all the beasts of chase*
> *That roam in woods of Caledon*
> *Crashing the forest in his race*
> *The mountain bull comes thundering on.*

In Swona – an island off Orkney which was evacuated in 1874 owing to the difficult conditions caused by its remote location – a small herd of black cattle was left, and has reverted to its wild state and cannot be safely handled.

The Calf Stone, carvings
Portmahomack Museum

As farming methods improved over the centuries, making it possible to provide some winter keep in the form of hay and straw (even holly and ivy were eaten as a last resort), cattle became the mainstay of the people, although it was not until the late eighteenth century that the turnip helped to reduce the animals' winter starvation.

Wealth was calculated by the number of cattle held, as it often still is today. A man owning sixty cows was a person of wealth in the eighteenth century. A girl's dowry was twenty milk cows for the daughter of a tacksman, while only a cow and calf for the daughter of a tenant. Cattle still make a girl's dowry in parts of Africa today.

Cattle were the source of wellbeing for the people of the Highlands, much as the buffalo were to the Native Americans and the reindeer were, and still are, to the Lapps of arctic Scandinavia.

From Medieval times until the early twentieth century a few cattle were housed under the same roof as the family during winter – the beasts in one end of the dwelling, their keepers at the other, often entering by the same door. The shared warmth was welcome and the morning milking was done in the comfort of indoors. With a slope on the floor, liquid waste found its way out, and the dung was then carted off to the midden.

As a provider of meat, milk, butter, cheese and clothing it is little wonder that the cattle beasts were cherished. And the oxen, of course, were also beasts of burden, which pulled the slype, the sledge, the wagon and the plough. Yoked in pairs, these castrated bulls with their slow steady movement were more reliable than the horse for ploughing. And they could stay longer in the yoke, while the horse was inclined to be restive and to need more feed. Oxgangs, a part of Edinburgh, refers to an area ploughed by oxen.

Columba was the patron saint of cattle, though it is

Oxen ploughing

said he was not keen on cows – as his monastery was an all-male establishment! I've no doubt his monks must have been glad of some milk, however, with butter and cheese perhaps supplied by the native people of Iona.

Bride was the patron saint of milkmaids and 1 February, St Bride's Day, marked the annual Milk Festival. This was when cows and ewes would be coming into milk and on this day every household would prepare a bed in the hopes that the saint would stay with their family.

As cattle were such an essential part of the life of Highland people, the whole of the year's work and activities was geared to the wellbeing of the animals. Two important festivals mark the care devoted to them.

At Beltane, on 1 May, they were driven between two ritual fires to rid them of evil spirits (and also of bugs!) on their way up to the summer grazings. At Samhain, now called Hallowe'en, they were welcomed back to their home ground. Each occasion was celebrated with feasting and fun.

CHAPTER TWO

The Caterans

AS CATTLE WERE BOTH the mainstay of the people and their form of currency, predators which could destroy the beasts were greatly to be feared. The wolf was a dire threat and the eagle could blind and even carry off a young calf. The greatest predator, however, was the human being – the *cateran*, or cattle thief, who could lift stolen cattle, known as a *creach*, in a stealthy dawn raid. Before the gradual break-down of clan society in the seventeenth and eighteenth centuries it was expected of a young, up-and-coming chief that he would make a raid on the cattle of another clan as proof of his manhood. Most often he chose a clan whose land was some distance from his own. He knew quite well, of course, that his victims would retaliate.

To carry off a *spreidh* of stolen beasts was an aristocratic pursuit said to date back to an ancient Indo-European custom. It was a tricky business, needing much skill and courage. The lie of the land would have been thoroughly investigated beforehand, perhaps through the clandestine activities of a spy. The cattle had to be driven warily, with the least possible disturbance, dogs quietened, men treading soft-footed till the track was reached. Even then not all danger was past, as those robbed might well have posted lookouts on the chance of a raid occurring. A moonlit night was most often preferred by the raiders. But 'Macfarlane's Lantern,' as the moon was known (the Macfarlanes being well-known caterans), could cast enough light that a gun-shot might reach its target. If the alert was sounded and the spreidh pursued, then a skirmish would ensue, with lives often lost before the cattle were turned back.

When stolen cattle were driven through the lands of a friendly clan on their way to the robber's, a share of the booty was demanded. This was known as *tasgan* money.

An instance of this came about in 1454 when members of the clan Munro in Easter Ross fell out with the Mackintoshes, through whose land at Moy they were driving stolen cattle, when they offered what was considered an insultingly small number of beasts as tribute.

The Mackintoshes pursued the Munros and on a hill about a mile to the west of Inverness, at Clachnaharry, a pitched battle took place. John Munro, having despatched the cattle to safety before the fighting began, was left for dead on the field but was rescued and revived by a woman who brought him to her chief, the lord of Lovat, who saw to his care. The battle is recorded in the Wardlaw Manuscript, written by James Fraser, cleric and historian, in 1666. Today a monument stands on the spot, with an inscription telling of the event.

Perhaps the greatest caterans were members of the clan Cameron of Lochaber. Their lands were rugged and unsuited to the rearing of good cattle, so the Camerons would travel miles, on foot or on horseback, in search of good stock and were quite ruthless in their handling of gun, sword, dagger or pistol if pursued.

A cateran with a romantic side to his nature was Donald Macdonald – 'Donald Donn,' brown-haired Donald of Lochaber. He was a man of a well-doing family, but he loved the adventurous life of cattle stealing. Handsome and brave, he was generous in his dealings and reputedly never harmed the poor or the weak. He was also a poet, which endeared him to many in his clan.

Once, when driving a spreidh of cattle in the Braemar area, he noticed an old woman hanging onto the neck of a cow he had taken. It was clear to Donald that creature was not only her livelihood, but the old lady loved it too. The cateran was taken aback. Reacting immediately, he released the cow from the herd and, to the woman's amazement, gave her another to take home along with it. News of his generosity spread amongst the people.

Returning home to Lochaber on another occasion from a raid in the north, Donald and his followers passed along the shores of Loch Ness. Here he met Mary, daughter of the laird of Grant, who lived in Urquhart Castle, and immediately fell in love with her. When her father heard of the cateran's feelings he forbade Mary to have anything to do with Donald, honourable man and poet though he was.

But Donald hid out in a nearby cave and would meet his love in the woods along the loch shore. Then, one day, receiving a message that Mary would meet him in a certain house, he went to the appointed place hoping there might

be good news from his love. He was given drink and told
that Mary would be with him soon.

But he had been betrayed. Sixty-three armed men of
clan Grant rushed in. He had no time to defend himself.
Escaping by a window, he ran for his life but was captured
and taken to the castle. There the chief, scowling, roared:
'tomorrow you will hang!'

Donald's answer was: 'The devil will take the laird o'
Grant out of his shoes and Donald Donn will not hang!'
Hanging was for common criminals. The chief eventually
agreed, at the request of his clansmen, to commute the sen-
tence to beheading. So, the following morning, on a hill
beside the castle, in front of assembled Grant clansmen and
his beloved Mary, he was beheaded.

In his last hours, as he was awaiting execution, he wrote:

Tomorrow I shall be on a hill without a head
And no one will have sympathy for me.
Have you no compassion on my sorrowful maiden,
My Mary, the fair and tender eyed?

Another sad happening involving caterans concerns a
banarach beag, a little dairy-maid. In 1644 soldiers disbanded
by the Duke of Montrose after the battle of Tippermuir
were on their way home to Glencoe when they came on
some fine fat cattle belonging to Colin Campbell of Glen
Lyon. Unable to resist the temptation, they proceeded to
drive the cattle off, along with the *banarach mhor*, the chief
dairymaid, who was tending them.

The little dairymaid, seeing what was happening, drove her charges, the calves, into a safe place, then set off quite fearlessly to trail the caterans with their booty, and to gather local people and show them the way the raiders had gone.

She had the cattle clearly in sight and was making headway when a shot rang out. She fell dead in the heather. A cateran lookout had seen a movement and reacted with his gun. On discovering he had shot a young girl he was remorseful, but the deed was already done.

When the men of Glen Lyon came on the body of the little dairymaid their anger spurred on their pursuit. Finding the caterans momentarily off guard they went for them with such ferocity with sword and gun that the robbers ran for their lives.

The banarach mhor, learning what had happened to her little companion, was heartbroken. A song she had been composing as she was taken away by the soldiers called 'Colin's Cattle' – *Crodh Chailin* – was sung in Glen Lyon on her return. It is about a fairy, whose cattle were the deer.

Colin's cattle would give their milk to my beloved,
On top of the moor without milking song or calf,
Brindled, speckled, spotted cattle, the colour of the grouse,
Cattle that would fill the milk pails and rear the calve,
The cattle of Colin, son of Conn,
Colin's cattle would give their milk to the heather.

It soon became famous. The song was adopted by a club

of distinguished men in Edinburgh which met regularly at a tavern in Anchor Close, kept by Daniel Douglas, whose favourite song it was. The frequenters of the tavern became known as the 'crochallans'. Robert Burns was a regular at the tavern during his days in Edinburgh and is known to have loved the song.

After the defeat of the Highland army at Culloden in 1746 many Jacobites, supporters of the Stuarts, who had been 'out' in the uprisings, were now 'out' in the heather, living as best they could, finding food and shelter among sympathisers, moving from place to place. Doubtless they took a cattle beast now and then, when deer proved elusive. The London government was totally ignorant of the ways of the Highland people, regarding them as savages. When their army of occupation came across a drove of cattle the Redcoats immediately assumed that the drovers were Jacobites and must be extirpated. The carrying of guns, along with the wearing of traditional Highland dress, had been banned after Culloden, the penalty for transgression being deportation for at least seven years. As a result, retaliation against the marauding Redcoats was almost impossible.

Fear of further uprising was very real in governmental minds. But life for the Highland people had to go on. Cattle would be 'lifted' in the traditional way, though perhaps on a smaller scale and with greater discretion.

It was the Redcoats who were in many ways the true savages – burning, pillaging, raping and killing their way through the Highlands. And it was the Redcoats who made the greatest depredations of livestock ever known in Scotland. Cattle, sheep, goats, horses, poultry – every living thing that would provide a meal or help with transport was appropriated. Much of this has been recorded – the quantity of spoil taken and the amount of compensation, if any, paid. Most often the compensation was ignored. At the barracks of Fort Augustus thousands of head of cattle were carried off from the surrounding counties to feed the troops.

Rob Roy MacGregor (Roy a corruption of the Gaelic *ruadh*, meaning red, or red-haired, as he was) began life as a cattle breeder, drover and dealer. A Highland warrior by descent, he had been 'out' in the rising of 1715 and taken part in the battle of Glenshiel in 1719. He was soon a marked man. His droving days now over, he became a cateran, taking cattle where he could, to eke out a living.

He devised a scheme of 'blackmail' (meaning 'illicit rent' in Gaelic), a protection racket, whereby he would receive payment for safeguarding a drover's cattle. MacGregor's watchmen were posted at strategic points, the leading raiders shot and the cattle restored to their original owners. This arrangement stood him in good stead when times were hard, such as after failed harvests and other disasters.

He never took from the small people, however, having his own code of honour. His clansmen respected him, though he was outlawed by the government. Depicted often as a rogue, he was never betrayed. Eventually, of course, he lost out, was imprisoned, escaped, then, reluctantly, came more or less to heel. He died, worn out, at the age of 63.

The habit of cattle lifting was finally brought to heel too. In 1727 General Wade, Commander-in-Chief of the Highlands, organised a vigilante patrol, composed of clan members loyal to the government, which would keep an eye on wandering Jacobites and also try to stamp out cattle raiding. They were called the Black Watch on account of the dark tartan they wore to make them inconspicuous on their nocturnal patrols. They were later formed into a regiment and fought for Britain overseas.

Old traditions die hard, but as the whole of Highland life was changing and a monetary economy taking over, so the accustomed ways were driven out. Emigration, the introduction of large numbers of sheep, and rules and regulations became the order of the day. Like the actions of Robin Hood and Ned Kelly, the deeds of the caterans became the stuff of legend and the subject of story-telling round many a ceilidh fire, as they still are today.

CHAPTER THREE

Summer at the Shielings

TRANSHUMANCE, THE SHIFTING of livestock to fresh ground at a certain time of year, was a practice common to communities in many parts of the world. In some places it still goes on. In the Highlands of Scotland, since very early times, cattle, horses, a few sheep and goats, and even some hens were taken up to the hill pastures in early summer when the grass was new and sweet. This migration took place around about the time of Beltane, after the cattle had been driven between the purifying fires. Some of them would be so weak after a long winter on scant rations that they had to be lifted and handled with care. They soon recovered after a few bites of fresh herbage, however, and would be ready for the trek to the hill pastures – the shielings, as they were known.

It was the women who coped with this sojourn in the wilds. With them went girls who would help with the dairying, some boys to herd the livestock, and perhaps one or two of the elderly men.

At the shieling ground there were one or more small dwellings, stone or turf-walled, thatched with heather, not unlike those of Iron Age people. One would be kept for the dairying, where the milk and cream could stay cool. The living places were sparsely furnished, with some benches and stools, and perhaps a cupboard in a recess in one wall. Beds were of heather and turf laid on the floor, within wooden frames, with blankets for a cover. A fire would serve cooking purposes and provide warmth on chilly evenings. On the eve of departure a celebratory meal was enjoyed as the excitement grew.

Duncan Campbell, who was editor of the *Northern Chronicle*, gives a wonderfully evocative picture of shieling life, in a paper read to the members of the Inverness Scientific Society and Field Club in 1895. Based on his own experience of life in Glen Lyon, he noted that some shielings were named after early saints and could once have been places where hermits sought solitude.

The 'big flitting' to the shielings was preceded by a 'small flitting', in which the men went to repair the summer houses after winter storms and to ensure that there was a store of peats to burn. When the day of departure for the big flitting dawned, the excitement was intense – children and dogs raced around, and even the cattle seeming to have an inkling of what it was all about. For some of them it might not have been their first visit to the uplands.

The women were anxious lest some essential item might be forgotten – as milk vessels, cheese presses, churns, pots, pans, spinning wheels, distaffs and spindles, flax, wool, meal, salt, blankets, clothing and many other items had to be packed into saddle bags, or onto light carts for the ponies to haul. At last they were off, but not before a blessing was invoked in song, such as the one Alexander Carmichael, the collector of traditional poems and songs, included in his book *Carmina Gadelica:*

Columba's Herding

May the herding of Columba
Encompass you going and returning
Encompass you in strath and ridge
And on the edge of each rough region

May it keep you from pit and from mine
Keep you from hill and from crag,
Keep you from loch and from downfall
Each evening and each darkling.

The peace of Columba be yours in the grazing,
The peace of Brigid be yours in the grazing,
The peace of Mary be yours in the grazing,
And may you return home safe-guarded.

A day would be needed for the journey to reach most shielings, although some were nearer to home. On arrival the first thing to do, even before the main unpacking, was to milk the cows. This was a job that could not wait. The animals might be restive after the journey, however, so their hind legs were sometimes tied together to keep them steady.

Then, when the men who had accompanied the flitting had had something to eat and a good drink of fresh milk, they would set off back home and shieling life would begin. The cattle and the goats would be put in the fold, a walled or wattle-fenced enclosure, while the horses might be tethered until they got accustomed to their new surroundings.

First thing in the morning the cows would be milked and the milk put into coggs (wooden containers) and shallow dishes on stone slabs in the dairy house. Scallop shells would be used to skim off the cream for butter making.

After milking the herd boys would drive the cows and other livestock to the hill grazings. It was a long day and a solitary one for the boys, but they passed the time happily enough, sometimes snaring a rabbit or guddling a trout for the pot. They gathered herbs too, for nourishment and medicine. Heather and thyme made health-giving drinks, nettles went into the broth and were rubbed on rheumatic knees, and the small yellow-flowered tormentil was used as a healer. Sometimes the boys worked away with a small sharp knife, making spoons, spirtles, milk whisks and other useful and attractive objects.

Soon the butter and cheese making would begin, the girls learning these skills as they watched the women. Butter could be buried in kegs in the peat to keep it fresh. Such kegs containing this 'bog butter', dating back several hundred years, have occasionally been found.

Cheese would often be smoked, hung from the roof timbers of the main house. A form of milkshake would be made by frothing up a cupful of milk with a little whisk. This was a favourite with the children and made the milk light and pleasant to taste on a warm day. Johnson and Boswell enjoyed such a drink at Shieldaig on their journey

to the Western Isles in 1773. Here is Boswell's account of
the day:

> 'At Auchnasheal we sat down on a green turf-seat at
> the end of the house: they brought us out two
> wooden dishes of milk which we tasted. One was
> frothed like a syllabub. I saw a woman preparing it
> with a stick as is used for chocolate.'

The girls soon became adept at the milking. They had
their favourites among the cows, and gave them names and
knew which songs to sing to them. A tune, they found,
made the milk flow readily. Thus:

> Lovely black cow, pride of the shieling,
> First cow of the byre, choice mother of calves.
> Wisps of straw round the cows of the townland,
> A shakle of silk on my heifer beloved.
> Ho my heifer, ho my gentle heifer.

There were many superstitions associated with cows.
Being so precious, the beasts had to be protected from evil
spirits. Red threads were sometimes tied to their tails and
rowan branches were hung above the door of the byre. The
bad spirits could even turn the milk sour if they were not
banished. Accusations of witchcraft were sometimes made
against those who indulged in these practices, but they
were only really indicative of the value placed on the cows
– animals which were a mainstay of people's lives.

The really good butter and cheese produced at the
shielings required the scrupulous cleaning of all the utensils

involved. They were of wood and had to be scrubbed with brushes of heather, in water heated by the plunging of hot stones into a pail. They were then set outside to dry in the sun and the wind. Shielings were always sited near a spring or a good-flowing burn so that a supply of water for all purposes was assured.

Some girls who did a lot of milking occasionally caught 'cowpox' – an inflammation akin to chickenpox – although it was said that this immunised them against the much more serious smallpox.

Next to dairying came other important work at the shielings – the spinning of wool and flax. On good days the women would sit at their wheels outside the door. Some of them still preferred to use the distaff and spindle, the original way of spinning, as they could work the wool while

Lochmaddy Tryst, North Uist, late 19th century
The Highland Council, Highland Folk Museum Collection

walking about, perhaps looking for herbs or for lichens which they used in dyeing the thread when they were done. Sitting too long they found irksome. Much flax was also spun at the shielings. It is a fine yarn and the long summer days provided the light necessary for the intricate work.

In older times life had not been so peaceful at the shielings. Duncan Campbell records how, on 20 August 1583, a band of Clanranald robbers – three score of them, armed with bows and other weapons – came at dawn to a shieling in Glen Lyon. On arrival they plundered huts, struck dairymaids and cut off the poor girls' hair. The raiders left with four score head of cattle, as well as eleven horses and mares.

Shielings that were near the droving routes would often provide shelter for the drovers and an overnight stance for their cattle when they passed in early autumn after the summer's occupants had gone home. In winter, fugitives were known to seek refuge in the shielings. The lairds sometimes took a turn up to the shielings to inspect the cattle and to enjoy a helping of milk or cheese.

One famous shieling visitor was Charles Edward Stuart – better known as Bonnie Prince Charlie. He was skulking in the heather after Culloden when a Jacobite guided him to a shieling hut in the hills of South Uist. Here Flora Macdonald, the Jacobite's sister, awaited the prince. She proffered a bowl of cream, as hospitality demanded, which he accepted gratefully. Then the famous journey to Skye was discussed. In later times the prince often took refuge in a shieling.

In 1719 the Assembly of the Church of Scotland had decreed that a schoolmaster should visit the shielings to instruct the herdboys in essential subjects. Girls, at that time, were not expected to receive instruction. A minister would also arrange prayer meetings at the shielings from time to time, as well as at the settlements where the men remained.

These men were kept busy at their own ploys. They would take the chance, when the family were away, to re-thatch the house. The old smoke-impregnated thatch made excellent fertiliser for the arable ground. They would also use the leather they had tanned to make new footwear for the winter. Some men went quarrying or burning lime. No doubt they would sometimes join forces with the men of the nearby settlements for an evening ceilidh and a dram!

At the shieling, too, life was not all work. There would be other shielings not far away, some within hailing distance. The young people would get together for a song and a dance on the green by the houses. Someone would have a pipe or a fiddle, or they could make 'mouth music' – humming in quick tempo – to dance to. The mothers would join in, remembering their youth. On wet nights there would be stories to tell.

Many lovely songs came from these happy days, when the herdboys cast eyes on the milkmaids.

> *Brown-haired girl I would choose you.*
> *Ho-ro you would be my choice.*
> *Brown-haired girl I would choose you,*
> *For sweetness and beauty.*

Brown haired girl of the fold
Young did I give you my devotions.
No other shall take you from me
Unless he wins you with gold.

There were also some sad songs by the lads left behind while their loves were away in the hills.

At some shielings small parcels of suitable, well-manured, land would be sown to oats or barley. Turf was cut for walling and some peats would be cut for use at home, although not too many, as the excavations could be dangerous for stock. At some shielings smelting was done too. Bog-iron could be found in the moss, and peat was available to heat a small furnace to extract the ore, using the basic technology of the time. The iron would make secure fastenings for tethered cattle.

By the mid-nineteenth century the pattern of life in the Highland communities was changing. Flax and then potatoes were being grown on a bigger scale. These crops were labour intensive, and needed much cultivation and weeding. This was work for women. Then came the introduction of large numbers of sheep, which were introduced in great quantity by impoverished landowners, as shepherds from the low-lands could pay substantial rents for grazing grounds. This meant that poor tenants, who could not afford the rents, had to remove their cattle and/or themselves. Gradually many shieling grounds were made over into sheep walks.

Meanwhile some areas were developed for sporting

purposes, spurred on by the growth of the railways and the access these gave wealthy businessmen to the Highlands, and used to support increasing numbers of red deer. A vogue for tree-planting also inspired land-owners in the late eighteenth and early nineteenth centuries, oaks and elms embellishing their driveways. The larch, a fast-growing conifer, was also introduced about this time. The Grants were great tree planters. They had established a flourishing timber trade on their Speyside estates and so enlarged their forests, thereby losing what had been good grazing ground.

Tenants were also being removed, in what became known as the Clearances, and many emigrated to the developing colonies – both through choice and by force.

As fewer shielings were occupied, the little houses were soon robbed of their stone walling to build dykes, sheep fanks, and butts for the shooters. Some were deliberately destroyed by landowners who feared they would attract vagrants.

In September 1803 Dorothy Wordsworth, writing in the journal she kept when on a tour of Scotland with her brother William, the poet, 'found several deserted mountain huts or shiels' near Loch Katrine, and 'a heap of scattered stones round which was a belt of green grass.' Such relics of the old shieling days can be seen today. That bright green grass grew where the cattle had trodden down weeds and had liberally manured the ground. Would that more cattle were doing the same today!

In the island of Lewis migrations to the shielings lasted

well into the twentieth century. The sites are still marked on maps today. Latterly some of the dwellings have been made into little holiday homes for the families who used them. With the walls lined, perhaps papered, windows made and bigger fireplaces installed they became attractive places to stay, situated as they were in the most beautiful areas. In some parts of the Alps, modernised shielings are still used for their original purpose, with a plastic pipeline taking milk to creameries in the valley below.

To return to our Highland shielings, as summer moved on and the grass began to lose its succulence, word would be sent to the men at the settlement that those on the high ground thought it was time to come home. The packhorses and the little carts would duly be driven up from the settlements and the shieling's stocks of butter and cheese, the lengths of woollen and linen material – all the produce of the summer days – would be stacked away safely for the return journey.

The cattle were fat and glossy, some of them destined for the long drive to the markets in the south, and the young people robust and ready for the winter and its long days in school. All were feeling the benefit of the fresh food and the hill air. The homecoming was celebrated with a meal and a ceilidh, and news would be eagerly exchanged with the folk of the settlement. Then, with everyone in good heart, all were ready to tackle the next big job – the harvest. The crops would be in good heart, too, barring storms, as the absence of the cattle, sheep and goats, even the

Orkney, early 1900s

hens, meant there were few destructive invasions during the growing season.

Walking the hill areas today and looking at those bright green patches where the cattle grazed, one wonders whether more high ground could be turned green – green and productive – by cattle grazing there and even by some sites being fenced off and cultivated?

Beside Loch Tay, where wonderful wild flowers now bloom, there were some fifty shieling sites indicating occupancy until the early nineteenth century. The remains of many little houses, some with recesses in the walls to form shelves of flagstones to keep the milk cool, can still be seen. The life that brightened them has gone, but the songs they inspired remain.

Traditional crofting in Drumbuie today, where wildflowers flourish, courtesy of the National Trust for Scotland

Brown-haired lass of the shieling
I would surely sit with you.
Brown-haired lass of the shieling
I would surely sit with you.
Brown-haired lass of the golden shieling
I would sit with you.
On the top of the high hills
And on the shieling of the hillocks.

Sung at a winter ceilidh, as it still is, this song brings back the magic of the long lost summer days.

CHAPTER FOUR

Droving

FROM EARLY TIMES, when livestock were first being kept and bred, domestic cattle and other animals would be taken to fresh pasture at certain seasons. A hazel switch was usually enough to put them on their way.

In Medieval times they would be taken to meeting places where exchanges with other breeders could improve the quality of the stock. The beasts would be driven along well-worn tracks to a point convenient for scattered communities to gather. Here, perhaps some stalls or booths would be set up for the exchange of goods or produce as well as livestock – wooden vessels, a snared rabbit, surplus grain, seed corn. The day would end with a drink, perhaps a song, and any differences would be sorted out before the drovers journeyed home.

The Industrial Revolution caused Highlanders to flock into the towns to work in factories. There was an increasing demand for meat to feed these landless workers and also to feed the men in the armed forces involved in Britain's Continental and maritime battles. Beef from the Highlands was especially prized and much of it was salted to feed the navy. Cattle – which had always provided meat, milk, butter, cheese, shoes and clothing for a family – now became the source of money for tenants to pay rent to their lairds and chiefs.

As a result, trysts, places where the sellers of cattle could meet, were set up at Muir-of-Ord, near Inverness, at Crieff in Perthshire, and at Falkirk. Crofters with only a few beasts for the market would sell them to a dealer who would make them up with other lots into a drove. Drovers sought safety in numbers, as caterans still lurked in the lonely passes and glens.

Drovers from the Outer Isles – the Uists, Benbecula, Barra, Lewis, Harris – would ferry the cattle to Skye, crossing the Minch from Lochmaddy in quite small boats. The islanders were first-rate sailors and there were boats everywhere. They would be lined with heather, small birch branches and bracken in order to prevent damage by the cattle's hooves. The beasts' heads would be tied to rings in the gunwales.

The crossing to the mainland from Skye was made at Kylerhea, and the cattle were often towed across to Glenelg roped head-to-tail behind the boats. It was a dangerous operation, among the currents and whirlpools, but, once ashore and washed clean after their swim, they would soon be fit for the long journey to the markets. Some drovers, however, preferred to ferry the cattle in boats.

Dealers from England would frequent the trysts at Falkirk and some drovers were encouraged to take their beasts further, to Carlisle, even East Anglia, where they could be fattened in the meadows, and even as far as London.

The journey, even as far as Crieff let alone London, was an arduous one. Some drovers set off in early summer, to allow their cattle to be fattened in the rich grazing of the

Swimming cattle across the Sound of Vatersay to Barra
Reg Allan, by kind permission of Frank G Thompson

south. But the main droves would set off in early autumn, ready fattened, for by September the cattle would be well-fed and strong after their summer grazing at the shielings.

Alexander Carmichael, the collector of folklore, found a herding blessing which might well suit the drovers as they set off:

Travelling moorland, travelling townland
Travelling mossland long and wide,
Be the herding of God the son about your feet
Safe and whole may ye safe return.

The sanctuary of Carmac of Columba
Be protecting you going and coming
And of the milkmaid of the soft palms
Bride of the clustering hair golden brown.

The drovers had to be hardy, loyal, lively and versatile. They had sometimes to act as vets, as well as to treat human ailments, to be able to handle money and to deal with awkward buyers. Some quite young boys often went with the drovers. They were quick to retrieve beasts which might have wandered from the track. Dogs, of course, were an essential part of the team. One or more ponies carried the leader and some baggage. Occasionally a man who merely wanted to travel to Crieff or elsewhere would accompany the drove.

A drove might consist of 100–200 beasts – a drover to every fifty or sixty. Sometimes the trail of cattle would stretch for five or six miles. They would cover not much more than twelve miles a day, with a rest at noon and a chance to graze and to drink. The drovers never forced the cattle to move faster or further. That would mean loss of condition. The Sabbath was respected and provided welcome rest for the men and their charges.

The drove roads, as the tracks came to be known, often followed the original pilgrim routes to sacred places such as Iona. They did not always go via the easiest routes, but often went over the high passes and through the lonely glens, before reaching the sea passages. The cattle did not like crossing water on a bridge, the noise of their hooves on

the hard surface alarming them. A man had to go ahead
with one beast on a rope, then the rest would follow, but
the cattle preferred to wade across the burns and rivers if
the water was not too deep.

At the end of the day the stance – a place known to be
sheltered, with good grazing and water – would be reached.
When the livestock was settled, the drovers could gather
thankfully round a fire of dry heather stems and sticks.
Their food was oatmeal, the staple ingredient of all their
meals, prepared as brose or porridge. They usually carried
onions and cheese too and a ram's horn of whisky. If in
dire need they would take some blood from the neck of a
young beast and mix it with oatmeal to make what we now
call black pudding.

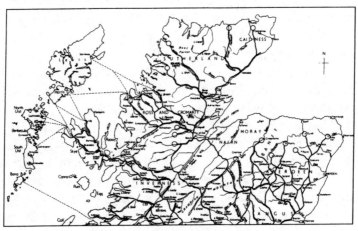

Map of the drove roads of Scotland
Birlinn Ltd, ARB Haldane

Night watchmen would take turns to keep an eye on the cattle. Some of the animals had a homing instinct but most were too tired to wander far. There was also of course the danger of raiders. The drovers mostly only carried a *sgian dubh*, or dagger, along with their sticks. They were, however, exempt from the Disarming Act of 1746 and so could also carry a gun, pistol or sword.

The heather made a springy bed. At some stances the bare ground had to suffice, but the men were hardy and accustomed to nights in the open. Even in September they sometimes awoke to find their plaids frosted or even covered with a sprinkling of snow. On the move early each day, they most often did not wait to make fire, but took their brose cold, washed down with a nip from the flask.

They seldom visited an inn for food or lodging, though hostelries lay near some parts of their route. Dorothy Wordsworth found Kingshouse on Rannoch moor 'filled with seven or eight travellers, probably drovers sitting in a complete circle round a large peat fire in the middle of the floor, each with a mess of porridge in a wooden vessel on his knee'. This was in 1803.

Here and there a friendly farmer might offer hospitality to the head man of the drove and feed the dogs. The stances provided a quantity of dung, from which nearby farmers would benefit. Today, like at the old shieling grounds, these stances are still visible as patches of bright green sward.

As the drovers passed by townships, as the settlements were known, people would welcome them as bearers of news from other parts. If, however, the cattle made depredations in cultivated land, as occasionally happened, they were far from welcome. In fact any beast found taking a mouthful of a precious crop awaiting harvest would be impounded, and payment then demanded for the animal's release.

Nearing the end of their journey, the drove would come to places where the dirt tracks were being turned into roads. The hard surface was hurtful to hooves accustomed to the soft moss and grass of the hill tracks.

As a result blacksmiths set up shops in several places where the 'made' roads were appearing. Here the cattle could be shod, with a specially shaped shoe. To shoe a three or four-year-old stirk (a heifer or bullock) was a trickier business than shoeing a horse. The animal had to be handled by three or four men, thrown on its back, then its legs bound.

Should a beast die on the drove, even after application of Archangel tar, the trusted pitch-like remedy for many ills, it had to be securely buried, so great was the fear of infection.

With the 'making' of the roads toll-booths were set up, where payment had to be made to allow the drove to pass. Finding this irksome, most of the drovers would avoid these contraptions, making detours over wild ground instead.

Many drovers carried goods to sell at the trysts – small handcrafted items, such as spoons, spirtles and plates. Some of them even knitted stockings as they rested or walked. Wearing silver buttons well hidden on an inner waistcoat was a way of ensuring appropriate burial should they die far from home.

The trysts were busy places. There were dealers with a practised eye always on the look-out for a good beast, auctioneers, pedlars shouting their wares, beggars hoping for scraps of food or money. And there were entertainers, jugglers, singers, story tellers for those with time to listen. It was a motley crowd – Gaelic, Scots, and English speakers haggling, arguing, joking and sometimes coming to blows.

The most important event, the selling of the beasts, was accomplished among the hubbub. Occasionally it happened that an expected price was not reached and the cattle had to be driven home. To men unaccustomed to handling cash the deals were mostly done with promissory notes, often merely pencilled figures scribbled on scraps of paper.

When Falkirk, which was nearer than Crieff to the southern markets, became the more favoured tryst in 1770 some 14,000 black cattle from the Highlands were sold there. By 1812 the number had risen to 80,000.

Tents were put up for the drovers. Banking booths did a great deal of business. The Royal Bank of Scotland, the British Linen Company and the Commercial Bank all issued bank notes in exchange for letters of credit – an improvement on the scraps of paper and an incentive to the furtherance of the banking system.

Some drovers, particularly single men, would stay on in the south, working at the harvests or doing other work on farms – ditching, walling, and using their various skills. They would then have some cash to take home, but would have to be wary in the more remote places as there were still plenty of vagrants around. Some dogs would be sent home on their own, while their masters stayed in the south to work. The wise beasts would remember the farms where they had been fed and on the next drove their owners would repay the kindly people who had cared for them.

Dogs were, of course, an essential part of the droving team – as was reflected by a 1873 drovers' dog show at Smithfield 'for the improvement of the breed of these useful animals and of their treatment' – although only the most experienced and intelligent dogs usually went with the drove. Several twelve- to thirteen-year-old boys usually accompanied the drove too, in order to learn the necessary skills. They were quick on their feet and able, like the dogs, to retrieve wandering cattle and keep the drove on track.

The drovers were welcomed in the places they came seeking cattle, in summer or in autumn. A Mackenzie from Loch Broom in Ross-shire composed a song about them:

What stout fellows
The drovers were when they got on the move,
Excellent, vigorous, lively lads they were
And full of ancient stories
And when they came to seek the cattle
They would not arrive empty-handed.
Oh, we liked the generous man
With his kilt and short hose
Who was typical of the best of the kind
He made it an expensive Whitsuntide for them.

There were many famous drovers. Perhaps best remembered is John Cameron, known as Corrychoile. He was born about 1780 in the parish of Kilmonivaig, near Spean Bridge. His father kept a toll-house, with an inn frequented by drovers. John would mind the stock while the drovers were in the inn. He saved what pay he got to buy a few sheep and goats to sell on. He went on to drive sheep and cattle, barefoot, to the Falkirk tryst. Scared of being robbed, he deposited money with the British Linen Company in Falkirk. Thus began his moneymaking days. Soon he was able to lease several farms on the Lochiel estate, where he could accommodate his growing numbers of livestock – horses, cattle and sheep.

As the years went by he became the largest holder of livestock in Scotland, perhaps even in all of Britain, having up to 50,000 beasts. His droves often stretched out over seven miles of roadway.

Corrychoile was only about five foot six but was wiry and had great powers of endurance. Travelling on a piebald pony he could cover 200 miles in less than two days, eating little and taking a drink of ale, which he also gave to his horse. Active into old age, though becoming impoverished, he was struck down suddenly and died in February 1856, aged seventy-five. Remembered as one who befriended less successful dealers, he was buried in the Roman Catholic graveyard of St Cyril's, Roy Bridge, where his headstone may still be seen.

With increasing levels of industrialisation, however,

new ways of transporting livestock were constantly being devised. In the quarterly journal of the Royal Highland and Agricultural Society of Scotland for February 1829 there is a description of a steamboat for carrying livestock. Peter Hedderwick, a marine architect from Leith, devised a scheme whereby, in a vessel of about 400 tons, cattle would be stalled, with the all-important ventilation assured. 'Stalls of sufficient size to hold with ease the fattest of the Highland cattle, taking them at about thirty or thirty two stone each,' claimed Hedderwick, 'and accordingly the vessel will carry 160 head, all properly stalled.' Stalls could be shifted, contracted or enlarged for cattle of smaller or larger size. Cattle could 'aggregate' safely in short passages, where 200 head could be held. Cattle would be hoisted on board in boxes or could be led if circumstances were favourable. Whether the vessel went into production is not recorded, so perhaps the cost was deemed prohibitive and the elaborate project was scrapped.

With the coming of the railways, taking cattle to the markets 'on the hoof' gradually ceased. The beasts were herded into cattle trucks and reached their destinations in a matter of hours, with time allowed for the animals to recover from the trauma of the trip.

Roads were greatly improved at this time and soon there was motorised transport available for livestock of all kinds. The frightened eyes of cattle seen through ventilation slots in the 'floats', as the trucks are known, give an inkling of what the beasts must feel, cooped up and in strange motion.

Landing cattle across the Sound of Vatersay to Barra
Reg Allan, by kind permission of Frank G Thompson

Though droving days in the Highlands were coming to an end by the late nineteenth century, the skills of drovers who had emigrated to Canada, America, Australia, and New Zealand were still very much in demand.

Murdo Mackenzie from Tain, in Easter Ross, went with his wife to Colorado in 1885. He became manager of the Matador Land and Cattle Company, which was based in Dundee. In America he never carried a gun and he banned drinking and gambling on the ranches under his supervision. He played the fiddle to keep the men, and himself, in good heart. In Texas, where he spent part of his career, a town is still called Murdo in his memory. Many a night as they sat round their camp fire his ranching men, known as cowboys, must have started up a Gaelic song remembered from their early days. The whole crowd would join in the chorus and a bout of mouth music, made for dancing, would banish nostalgia and bring laughter and cheers.

Some cowboys did go wild and allowed the cattle to run amok, and many animals were lost in blizzards. The need for fencing and some winter feed had to be accepted. In 1874 barbed wire was first used on the ranches. The ways of droving were changing with the enclosures and with the prairies being settled by incomers, causing a certain sadness among the cowboys. One nostalgic song went, and still goes, like this:

I'm going to leave old Texas now,
They've no more use for the long-horned cow.
I'll take my horse, I'll take my rope
And hit the trail upon a lope.

The ground at night will be my bed,
My saddle-seat beneath my head.
And when I waken from my dreams
I'll eat my bread and my sardines.

And when my work on earth is done
I'll take my chance with the Holy One.
I'll tell St Peter that I know
A cowboy's soul ain't white as snow
But in that far-off happy land
He sometimes acted like a man.

The long-horned cattle popular in North America had been brought in by immigrants, probably the Spanish in early times. They were valued for their flesh and also for their horns, which made useful domestic articles. These horns could, however, be a danger, particularly in stampedes. Also, in the late nineteenth century, cattle from Texas were said to carry the germ of a fever.

In Australia there was also much ranching of cattle, and there the Highland immigrants proved their worth. Sheep were more numerous, however, and the Highlanders soon learnt to work with them, though shepherding was not really in their blood. A few sheep would disappear when times were hard. They never did like large numbers of those great white-faced sheep!

So the long, slow droving days of the Highlands are long gone, though their stories, songs and legends are alive in many minds. Selling beasts by auction with farmers and dealers coming from far and wide to the 'marts' is now the norm. Cattle are taken to the selling point, paraded in the ring, and the buyers arrange transport thereafter.

In the late twentieth century young male calves were being exported in large numbers to meet the demand for veal in Europe. Happily, this was quite soon prohibited as significant cruelty was incurred in the cramped transport of the calves.

Although the trysts are no longer, summer still brings livestock shows to places large and small. The beasts are groomed till their coats glisten and there's a shine on horn

**Cattle walking on the road, Alastair White,
early 1930s**

View from Strathrory Drover's Road overlooking farmland and forest
© Jude Dobson and licensed for reuse under this Creative Commons Licence

and even hoof. All this in pursuit of a gaudy rosette, a little plaque in the byre and a trophy for the owner's sideboard! But a good day is still had by all, especially the farmers, who can admire, compare and argue as they always do. The beasts are glad to get home though, to trudge uninhibited once more through the mud.

Today the old drove roads, those that were not made into stone-lined routes by General Wade and his soldiers, make wonderful ways for walkers and riders. They go through those beautiful high passes and deep glens. Many are signposted, with distances indicated and warnings about altitude! Walking them, one can almost enter into the drover's life.

CHAPTER FIVE

Hide, Hair, Horn and Hoof

SINCE HUMANS EMERGED FROM CAVES, began to move in a wider world and to make the means of killing animals, they soon found a use for the skin, as well as the flesh, of dead creatures. Though the ice had gone, the world was still a chilly place. There were not many furry, woolly beasts around, but the skin of the aurochs would provide cover for a whole family. To kill such a large animal was not easy, but eventually, after frantic effort, stalking and skilful targeting, they could manage, with spear and arrow, to overcome an unwary beast. To skin it, and cut the skin to fit, was another arduous task with the tools available – flint knives, sharp as they were. The meat would give strength to a whole community.

As the years and the centuries passed other beasts – such as deer, sheep, goats and beaver – also provided skins. Aurochs, tamed and now called cattle, still provided skins for clothing, however. At New Year, until last century, boys would visit the houses and dance about draped in a bull hide. The strength of the beast would, they hoped, permeate their own skin and make them into heroes.

Soon the early people began to explore their wider

territory, where trees were growing into dense forests. Ways through the thickets were few in the wild country of the north. But there was water, never too far away. The sea was on the islanders' doorstep, while on the mainland rivers and lochs abounded. As a result, the people of both the islands and the mainland soon became skilled navigators.

Dug-out canoes made travel possible on river or sea. The making of them needed much labour – cutting down the trees, as they watched the beaver doing, and then hollowing out the trunks. Then someone had the idea of fashioning a craft from ox or cow hide. It had proved waterproof and malleable in the uses to which it had already been put, the making of clothing and containers for water. So a skin was processed in the usual way – soaked, scraped, made pliable, then fixed into a framework of branches – and the curragh was born.

Small curraghs were still in use in Highland rivers until the twentieth century. They were ideal for poaching expeditions, as they could be lifted and carried off quickly should a wary gamekeeper approach. In the museum at Elgin, in Morayshire, a vessel of this type can be seen.

In the early eighteenth century Alasdair Mor Grant, who was his chief's ferryman and 'champion' (head servant), was said to have walked to London with his curragh on his back. He launched it on the Thames, and people, thinking it belonged to a beggar, threw coins into it. He later presented the money to his chief, asking him to buy some 'pins' for his lady wife!

Much bigger boats were also built of the same materials, some carrying sails which were also made of hide. Brendan sailed to the far north in one of these craft, possibly all the way to North America. Columba and his followers also used them to reach Iona and the Scottish mainland from Ireland, thus making them an important factor in the spread of religion to these isles.

With the coming of Christianity and the establishment of various monasteries, the monks began to spend many hours copying the gospels and transforming them into amazing works of art. Their quills were goose feathers, most of the colours came from local plants and their wonderful illustrated texts were written on the skin of calves, known as vellum.

More martial means were served by the skins of cattle too, as time passed and more sophisticated modes of fighting went on between the clans – groups whose quarrels were mostly over possession of land or for avenging insults. Protective shields were devised which could bear the brunt of opposing spear, arrow or sword attack. These were made of cow hide stretched on a wooden frame with a sharp spike in the centre.

Sporrans, bags for the carrying of meal or other food-stuffs and hung from the waist, were also made of hide, as was footwear – brogues as they were known – although most people travelled barefoot until relatively recently.

Harnesses for horses or oxen and saddle-bags were made of hide and it had many domestic uses, including making bowls and drinking vessels. It could also be made into sieves by piercing holes in the hide with red-hot skewers.

New skills in the fashioning of the material were continually being acquired and improved. Tanning, making skin into leather, was an elaborate process, using a solution of oak bark or the roots of tormentil, with much scraping, soaking and stretching to make for pliability. In post-Medieval times the demand for leather was so great that commercial tanneries were set up. In Inverness an export trade to Holland and other European countries was established.

The coarse outer hair of the cow could be combined with the soft under-hair to produce a yarn. This could be woven or felted. The strands of the tail could also be used to make rope.

Every part of the animal had a use or uses. The horn was especially valued. Made into a drinking vessel it was superb. The chief of Macleod, at his investiture, had to drink half a gallon of claret, in one go, from the famous Dunvegan drinking-horn. He also sported a waistcoat of ox hide. Horn made snuff mulls too, thus being part of another happy habit of the time!

It was also used as part of the ever-changing ways of warfare, as a powder horn, often adorned with the owner's name and regiment, inscribed during the wearisome hours waiting for the fighting to begin.

A cow horn made one of the first musical instruments. To be 'put to the horn' meant that, after three blasts on the instrument, a man was declared an outlaw. Sliced thinly,

Single cattle. A lonely Highlander
© Roy Dennis

horn was translucent and was used, like glass, in small lanterns. Scholars had horn books, the leaves held between two flat sheets of the substance. Early prayer-books were also made in this way by the monks.

Horn plates were put in jerkins for protection against arrows or lance thrusts. Ornaments were made of carved horn. Today some craftspeople are using their skills to work with horn again.

More mundane uses of horn were many. It made buttons, combs, knife-handles, and spoons. The travelling people were particularly skilled at making the latter. They made a mould for the softened horn, keeping the exact method used a secret. When the horn was heated to make it flexible it was split, the inner substance boiled for fat and made into soap and axle grease. The liquid was then boiled down to make glue.

What house, even in recent days, did not have a shoe-horn in the porch ready to ease a tight shoe onto a delicate foot? Plastic has not the same feel, nor the same gentle shape.

The medics of older times, indeed until the late twentieth century, found a use for a horn. The open end would be placed over a swelling, say, in a joint, pressure applied and the swelling's liquid would move into the horn, thus relieving pain. This procedure, known as cupping, was widely used in the Highlands.

The hoof, particularly the calf's foot, provided a substance used to make a jelly. I well remember being given, when a child, calf's foot jelly as a tonic after measles or whooping-cough. It could also be used as a dessert. Mrs Beeton, of cook-book fame, has six recipes for variants of the dessert theme. She should know! Here is one of her recipes for calf's foot broth:

To make 4–6 helpings you need – 1 calf's foot; 1.5 litres of water; 2–3 strips lemon rind; salt and pepper; egg yolks; and milk.

Wash the foot thoroughly. Put in large pan with water, heat to simmering gently for 3 hours. Strain through colander or sieve into basin. Leave to cool. When cold skim fat. Reheat with lemon. Season. For 250ml allow 1 egg yolk and 4 x 15 ml spoons of milk. Beat together egg yolks and milk. Beat into hot soup.

The fat of oxen was used to make tallow, much in demand in the eighteenth century for the candles used to grace those chandeliers which adorned the big houses of the time. In some places cattle were fattened especially for the production of this valuable substance.

The bones of cattle must not be forgotten. Oxtail stew is a meal to remember, and marrow bones make a satisfying soup. Long, slim scoops can also be used to extract the marrow. Eat it as it comes or put it on toast! Bones were ground and mixed with fine clay to make bone china too. Remember that when your lips meet the delicate rim of your teacup!

As the cow, the bull and their offspring were so vital in the lives of the Highland people it is small wonder that, when their cattle were driven off in the late eighteenth century in favour of the huge flocks of alien sheep, riots ensued.

1792 was known as the 'Year of the Sheep' due to the high rate of tenant evictions, as the Highland landlords increasingly favoured farming the animals at the expense of their traditional crofting tenants. In response to this worrying trend the people of Strathrusdale in Easter Ross got together to drive all the sheep, put down by Camerons from Lochaber, out of the area where their cattle grazed.

The alarm among the powers-that-be was such that troops from Fort George were sent in to quell the riots. Several ringleaders were arrested, one sentenced to deportation to Botany Bay, two banished from Scotland for life and one fined a colossal sum that he could never repay. However, awaiting their sentences in Inverness, the troublemakers found the door surreptitiously opened. They escaped and were never heard from again.

In 1882, in the Braes area of Skye, farmers refused to pay their rent when their cattle were turned off their grazings, so a squad of police from Glasgow was sent to enforce payment. Most of the men were away at the fishing, but the women and children, armed with sticks and stones, took to the hills and flung boulders at the police. Several of the squad were quite badly hurt and eventually retreated back to Portree. This encounter became known as 'The Battle of the Braes'. A roadside plaque now commemorates the event.

Meanwhile in the north of Skye, in Glendale, the crofters refused to pay rent until the grazing for their cattle was restored. In 1883 gun-boats were brought in containing marines and armed police. Several men were arrested and imprisoned in Edinburgh. On their release they became known as the 'Glendale martyrs'.

'Illustrated London News' 1883
Contemporary illustration of the Battle of the Braes in Skye, as the tenants began
to resist the excesses of the landlords. But at least some sections of
Scottish public regarded the Gaels as lazy and feckless, to be cleared out to
make way for more "moral, industrious and frugal" peoples

When sheep became less profitable, owing largely to competition from Australia and New Zealand, deer took over the grazings in order to provide sport. The hungry animals also destroyed crofters' crops, leaping fences and dykes at will.

The result of all this mismanagement can be seen today, where acres of rushes and bracken despoil the land once kept in good heart by the treading and grazing of the cattle beasts, those same cattle that would have come at a call when a mile distant from home. If the bright green patches of the shieling grounds could spread over a whole hillside what a different country we would see.

Cattle provided everything a community needed. Even the dung served several purposes. A cow would produce about four tons of dung a year. In the well-known 'cow-pats' insects would flourish, which fed birds. The chough – that interesting red-legged member of the crow family – depends almost entirely on this prime fare. This recycling of nutrients is positive and of immense value. Dried, the dung could also be used as fuel, as it is in Africa today.

It is clear that the people were ready to risk serious injury, even death itself, in the struggle to preserve their cattle-based existence. While most farmers had always kept a few sheep – small hardy creatures, which gave fine wool for the making of garments, and which they milked to make cheese – the incoming Cheviot breed were huge, with huge appetites. These grazed everything bare, souring the ground as they roamed. The people hated them, their hatred finding expression in incidents such as the Battle of the Braes as well as the skilled satire of their bards.

This was in stark contrast to the crofters' love of their cattle. Even today, in the shine on the faces of those appraising cattle in the field or the show-ring, you can sense the regard and affection in which these comely beasts are still held.

CHAPTER SIX

In the Kitchen

MILK WAS PERHAPS THE MOST essential item in the diet of the Highland people over many centuries. It provided food – butter and cheese – and drink in many forms. It is no wonder that the 'milch' cows were given names, were petted and were allowed any spare feed that was available in winter. They were also the subject of numerous songs, such as one Alexander Carmichael found in Barra:

Come, Mary, and milk for me my cow,
Come Bridget and encompass her now
Come o Columba kindly enow,
And twine thy two arms around my cow.
Ho my heifer, my lovely heifer
Ho my heifer, ho lovely heifer
Heifer my heart, kind, loving ever.
To thy calf o take
For the high king's sake.

The last lines refer to the fact that sometimes the cow had to be persuaded to allow the calf to suckle.

During the worst months of the year, and in the time before calving, the cow's milk would dry up. Some goats were kept and there were ewes around, hardy creatures who could quite often supply milk to fill the gap. Ewe's milk was also used to make cheese.

When the 'house' cow – the animal used to provide milk for the family – calved, there was great rejoicing. In the build-up to calving the family would wonder whether the calf was a female or a male, a heifer or a bull? The excitement grew as calving drew close. If she was a heifer, that put a smile on every face, for she would be a milker in days to come. If he was a bull calf, well, that was fine too, as he would grow into a bullock to go on the drove.

The calf suckled the first milk which was rich in special nutrients. Thereafter it was fed from a pail and the cow was milked twice, sometimes three times, daily. A sup of the new milk would be sent to a neighbour who had none.

After the family, especially the children, had had a drink of the precious 'white stuff' the rest would be poured into flat dishes in a cool place, perhaps in the closet – the small cool room in the middle of the house, situated well away from the fire. With the improvement in housing in the late nineteenth century, an extension would be built on to the back of the dwelling. This was known as the milk house and would have shelves of slate or stone which kept the milk cool.

When the cream had risen in the milk dishes, it would be skimmed off, often with a scallop shell, for the making of butter. This was made in a wooden plunger churn, which consisted of a narrow, staved vessel, with a hole in the lid through which the plunger, a stick with a cross-piece on the end, was thrust. This plunger was worked briskly up and down until the cream solidified into butter. Later the rotary churn, with paddles, made for an easier job. Today churns are of glass or metal. A small quantity of butter could be made by shaking the cream in a bottle – shaking and shaking till the butter came. Carmichael records the process in the 'Charm of the butter':

> *Thou who put beam in moon and sun*
> *Thou who put food in ear and herd*
> *Thou who put fish in stream and sea*
> *Send the butter up betimes.*
> *Come ye rich lumps, come!*
> *Come ye rich lumps, come!*
> *Come ye rich lumps in masses large,*
> *Come ye rich lumps, come!*

That charm would surely do the trick!

Hard cheese was made in presses weighed down with heavy stones. This needed a large quantity of cream and the process took both time and strength. The cheese would be kept for several months and was a very important part of the diet.

Cheese and oatcakes were served at the end of the laird's dining table for the lower orders. On every social occasion it was enjoyed – at wedding feasts and at baptisms. It gave strength to the coffin-bearers at a funeral and it made a midday meal for the peat-cutter, the drover, the herdsman, the traveller and anyone who was far from home.

At one with the hills
© Roy Dennis

On nearly every farm a soft cheese was regularly made, as it had been since very early times. The method was simple. A bowl of milk was left in a warm place until it soured. The curd was cooked slightly. When the whey (the liquid) separated and ran off, the solid was put into a bag of muslin and perhaps hung outside on the branch of a tree until all the whey had drained out. Spread on an oatcake with a spoonful of blackcurrant jelly, this crowdie, as it was called, was a meal to remember. Surplus crowdie could be mixed with butter, packed in crocks and sealed with a layer of butter. The crocks could be kept in a cool place, perhaps even in the barn, for use during the winter.

A richer soft cheese, originally meant for clan chiefs, is being re-invented today in Tain, Easter Ross. It is made with double cream and rolled in pinhead oatmeal. Called 'caboc' from the Scots word 'kebbuck', meaning a round cheese, it is a real delicacy which is well worth a try.

A sweet dish could also be made from curds by adding rennet to make it set, then sugar and cream. This was known as white pudding and was popular with children. The most delicious of all Highland desserts, however, must be crannachan. To 3–4 ounces of pinhead oatmeal add half a pint of half whipped double cream, a spoonful of whisky and soft fruit. Honey can be added if liked. This dish was often served at Hallowe'en with a small charm hidden in it. Once tasted, it is never forgotten! Milk drinks were many and various. Whey and buttermilk were considered health-giving and were drunk in large quantities. Remember Little Miss Muffet?

In eighteenth century Edinburgh dairymaids from the country would ride in on horse-back, pails dangling from their saddle-bags. They would sell the whey at a penny a pint, from a favourite stance at the Tron church.

A milkshake, as we call it today, would be made by frothing up a beaker with a 'fro-stick' – a stick with a cross-piece on the end which was worked up and down till the milk bubbled up. This made a pleasant and health-giving drink, much enjoyed, especially by children. Atholl brose was another much prized drink. This is made by mixing heather honey with water in which oatmeal has been steeped, together with cream and whisky. This can be enjoyed today, strictly by adults!

Johnson and Boswell, during their Highland tour of 1773, were often surprised at the amount of milk and milk dishes they found everywhere. Without the refrigeration and transport facilities we have today it had, of course, mostly to be consumed on a daily basis.

One way of using buttermilk (the liquid left after churning the butter) was to mix it with fresh milk (two pints to one), heat the mixture, then pour it into a bowl and leave overnight. On the next day, drain off the whey, add sugar to the curd, whip half a pint of cream and mix together. This dish was known as 'hatted kit' – worth making for the name alone!

What we call today 'butcher meat' was very little used in the smaller households of the Highlands. Beef was of most value on the hoof. Should an animal suffer injury and have to be destroyed then every part of the carcass, from horn to tail, would be used. A piece of meat would be added to the broth of vegetables and barley, then eaten separately with potatoes. Stew would be made and minced collops (mince). Steaks and roasts were for the big house, where cooking facilities were much greater. Some meat would be salted for winter use.

Black puddings were a source of protein when meat was in short supply. Blood would be taken from the neck of a young beast. A bleeding knife, known as a fleam, was used, which had several blades for cutting at different depths.

The blood, mixed with oatmeal and onion, made a tasty and nourishing meal. So highly prized was the black pudding that a man would sneak out at night to poach blood from another's beast if he had none of his own available. On one occasion a man caught doing this was accused of witchcraft when all he wanted was to provide nourishment for his desperately ill wife. Today we can buy black puddings at the butcher's or the supermarket, minus the romance!

So important were milk and its derivatives of butter and cheese, that it could even take the place of oatmeal in the diet, when this was scarce or dear after a bad harvest.

It also had curative properties and was used to help sufferers from various ailments. To be bathed in milk was not part of a beauty treatment as it might be today, but was said to ease the pain of arthritis, to cure skin diseases, and even – it was believed in early times – leprosy. Such a treatment could only be done when milk was plentiful, however.

The Celtic hero Cuchulain was cured of an unspecified affliction, perhaps depression, from which he did indeed suffer, when bathed in milk, so the legend goes – one of the many legends that contains a spice of truth!

Goat's, ewe's, mare's and even hind's milk were also used in remedial measures.

A beaker of hot cow's milk with a dash of rum, taken at bedtime, was always a welcome and effective means of warding off a cold. Better than a toddy any day!

Butter mixed with oatmeal made an excellent poultice

for the relief of swellings. Buttermilk was used for skin irritation, for sunburn and even just for washing the face.

At one time butter was part of the rent in kind due to the chief. Later it could be sold at the fairs. Shaped with butter pats, bearing an attractive and ingenious moulded stamp, it was a precious commodity, used as currency. Cheese was also used in this way.

Before the introduction, in the twentieth century, of chemical fertilisers and pesticides (known to the crofters as 'artificials'), dung, seaweed and sooty thatch were the natural improvers of the ground, so people's diets were organic and healthy. In many ways it was similar to that advocated today, particularly by vegetarians. Many of the quite expensive products sold now in health shops were available for the gathering.

Nuts are full of protein, wild fruits a source of vitamins, and seaweed contains iodine. The women were knowledgeable about the uses of wild herbs. Over the centuries, through a long process of trial and error, knowledge of the use of herbs for nutritional and medicinal purposes gradually grew. Thankfully many herbs need only scant soil and whatever sunshine is going. Thyme, sage, garlic, lovage, parsley and mint were all used, as were many flowering plants and berries.

It is to be hoped that some of this knowledge will be picked up by the younger generation now showing an interest in such things and that the over-enthusiastic use of artificials will not destroy the natural sources of nourishment. And let us keep the white stuff coming!

CHAPTER SEVEN

Cattle in Story and Song

THE CLOSE RELATIONSHIP between humans and cattle is demonstrated by the numbers of songs and verses that mention the beasts. These came largely from the people most closely involved with the cows and calves – the women. For, during the milking, the women would be in daily physical contact with the cow.

And, while the people spoke and sang to the cattle, the cattle themselves sometimes tried to communicate with their keepers. The cows, for example, even have an engaging habit of letting us know when they are feeling like a bit of a fling!

As they bellow their warning they are roped, just to keep them on the straight and narrow, as we lead them, or they lead us, to the domain of their favoured bull. We can then calculate the expected time of arrival of their next off-spring and the ensuing full supply of milk. At Caiplich, during the necessary drying-off period before calving, we had to make do with what the goat could give us or buy the odd tin of Carnation, while our cow was petted and given titbits of her favourite food.

Of course, we humans have always been fond of our cows and see them as the fount of all goodness. Some are almost members of the family and so are often given names – such as Mairi, Bella, Bess, Maggie and Dolly. Their ways, their quirks, their likes and dislikes are all studied and it is from this close contact that so many songs spring.

From Mary MacNeill, milkmaid to the MacNeills of Barra for fifty-five years, came 'My Brown Cow' – a song which my cow would have loved, one of the many she sang. It sounds even better in Gaelic.

Ho, my little cow, ho my brown cow,
Ho, my little cow, ho, my brown cow.
Little cow of my heart, dear beloved.
Thou seekest not calf, nor calfling of me.
Ho, my little cow, ho, my brown cow
Ho, my little cow, ho, my brown cow.
My sweet little cow, dear beloved,
With me thou wouldst cross the crest of the waves.

There were songs for all aspects of farming cattle – the churning, the making of cream into butter, the pressing of cheese, and for all the processes of turning the precious milk into sustenance. Sometimes it happened that the cow would not take to her calf. This could be a calamity. In such a case a milking croon might have been sung by a young woman at the shielings, out in the summer air.

Come, Brendan from the ocean,
Come Ternan, most potent of men.
Come, Michael valiant, down
And propitiate to me the cow of my joy.
Ho, my heifer, ho heifer of my love.

Ho heifer, ho heifer of my love.
My beloved heifer, choice cow of every shieling
For the sake of the high king, take to thy calf.
Come beloved Colum of the fold,
Come, great Bride of the flocks
Come, fair Mary from the cloud
And propitiate to me the cow of my love.
Ho, my heifer, ho heifer of my love.

Once, on Iona, a poor little woman, whose husband and son had drowned, leaving her with three orphaned children, came to seek advice from Columba. Her lovely little heifer would neither give milk nor take to her calf. What was the woman to do?

Columba would know, she thought – as he was the font of all wisdom and the 'head of healing' – but the saint told her he had lost his little book of charms for the healing of cattle and horses. However, he conceded, 'I will make a rune for thee, poor little woman, which thou shalt sing to thy heifer and before thou shalt have finished the rune the heifer will have taken to her calf.' And so Columba duly wrote the rune:

My heifer beloved, be not alone,
Let thy little calf be before thee.
See yon bramble bush a-bending
And bowing down with brambles.
He-ho-li – vo's a vó ri ag
Ri ag vó, take to thy calf

Coax thy pretty one to thyself
Till thou sendest to the fold a herd
Columba's tending shall be thine behind them,
He made this lilt for thyself.

Even more verses followed. The little woman sang them all and the heifer allowed the calf to suckle, the precious milk flowing free.

In Colin Macdonald's book *Echoes of the Glen* there is an extraordinary, but true, story of the attachment of a crofting family to its house cow. When *bho ruadh* (the red cow) reached a certain age, it was decreed that she must be sold to make way for a younger beast. Though she was lean, with a silken skin, she had to go. However, because she was almost part of the family, they sent her not to any old drover, but to a gamekeeper in a lonely glen, some twenty miles away, who they knew would treat her well. There was 'a load of sorrow' on the house that day.

Early next morning the family awoke to the sound of the dog barking furiously. Then came the bellowing of a cow. 'That sounds like bho ruadh, but it can't be!' Colin rushed out, barefoot. 'It is!' he yelled. 'She's standing at the byre door waiting to be milked!' And so she was, having tramped the twenty miles home.

Herding the cattle, in the days before fields were fenced, making sure they couldn't snatch a bite of corn or turnip on their way to the grassy hollows where they would graze the day away, was work allocated to the boys in each community. The animals were biddable enough – I've seen a four-year-old shift a group of stirks with just a wave of a tiny hazel switch – but watching the beasts all day could be a dull and lonely job and some of the boys suffered as a result.

One young herd-boy on Iona, for example, came to Columba to seek help when he began to suffer from depression from spending so much time on his own. Columba, with his experience as a healer, knew that in the armpit several nerve-endings met. He rubbed the boy's arm with a salve made from St John's Wort. This plant became known as 'Columba's armpit flower.' It must have done its job, for it can still be found in health shops today.

Herding could sometimes be dangerous on difficult

Highland Cattle at Blacklunans
Robert E Fuller

ground, so a blessing, such as the following, was often invoked:

Travelling moorland, traveling townland
Travelling mossland long and wide
Be the herding of God the son about your feet,
Safe and whole may ye home return.
The sanctuary of Carmac and of Columba
Be protecting you going and coming
And of the milkmaid of the soft palms
Bride of the clustering hair golden brown.

There were other, more outlandish, tales to emerge from the herdsmen and herdsboys. One such boy, who had been herding cattle in a lonely place in the hills above Loch Ness some sixty years ago, rushed into the kitchen one evening to tell his mother he had seen 'some little green folk' among the rocks by the burn. His mother gave him a good skelp for telling lies, but he stuck to his story all his days, even when he became an army chaplain serving in India.

Had he nodded off that warm day, in spite of the midges? Did he dream a dream? It's true that some of the old folk, in those days, would leave out a dish of porridge at night for the 'wee folk'. It always disappeared, but down whose throat no one knew.

A little magic is good for the soul!

In his 1947 book *Croft and Ceilidh* Colin Macdonald has a remarkable story about Ruairidh Mor an Drobhair – Big Rory the Drover. Colin got the story from a friend whose mother knew a man who was a lad in 1745. Old age and memory played a marvellous part in his story-telling.

Big Rory, so the story goes, had droving in his blood. Every September he would buy up all the marketable beasts in the area and take them to the Falkirk tryst. Sometimes they sold well, sometimes not, but he was always honest in his deals.

One time he was lucky. For the 150 beasts he sold he made a big profit, so had a large sum of money in his sporran. The long journey home would be risky, for bandits lurked in the hills, so he was careful not to mention his luck to anyone. Indeed, he tried instead to make out he had done badly at the tryst.

Approaching the Bealach Gaibh (the Rough Pass) – a dreadful dark place, surrounded by towering cliffs and littered with huge boulders – he decided to stop for the night at the inn at Clachan, near Drymen, to fortify himself for the journey ahead. As he was drinking, three sinister-looking strangers arrived. Concerned for his well being, Big Rory feigned drunkenness and staggered off to bed, but not to sleep.

Leaving the inn by the back door he avoided the pass, where he knew the sinister newcomers would look for him, and made over into the next valley instead. He was exhausted. Then he remembered a quarry where he could get shelter and have a sleep. Reaching it he was amazed to find the glowing embers of a fire, where an old friend of his was sitting. They drank together happily till an incautious remark turned their friendship to fury.

Rory made off and had a sleep in the shelter of a rock, but soon awoke with the cold. Making back to the quarry and the fire, he lay down beside his recumbent friend. Wakening with daylight he was amazed to find blood on his hands and clothes. The friend lay dead beside Big Rory in a pool of blood, his head smashed in. Terrified, Rory made off at speed, only to run into a poacher. After washing himself in a burn the drover finally reached home, exhausted, and told his wife of his good fortune at the market, news which she spread proudly around.

Meanwhile, the poacher had been to the quarry, found the dead man, remembered the fear in Rory's face, put two and two together and soon the big drover was accused of murder and sentenced to be hanged.

At the last moment a young man galloped up to the gallows. He had been near the quarry on that fateful night, where he'd met a lone tramp. The tramp was traced and found to be in possession of a knife and a snuff mull belonging to the murdered man, as well as a large sum of money, so Rory was set free. Yet, this was only one of the many misadventures suffered by the big drover.

Many another drover – in the wild times – experienced loss, injury and even death. It was not a job for the faint-hearted. In the fifteenth century the persistent lifting of cattle by the Camerons of Lochaber led to tragedy and disaster on an epic scale.

For, on one occasion, Lochiel, chief of clan Cameron, sailed off to Ireland with a large retinue of clansmen – in order to visit, and impress, some of the Irish chiefs. Meanwhile Hector Maclean, egged on by the Lord of the Isles and emboldened by the absence of so many Cameron warriors, pillaged Lochiel's lands in revenge for many years of Cameron raids.

Maclean not only took every cattle beast, but every horse, sheep and goat, as well as armaments and even store corn. After some sporadic fighting, with casualties on both sides, Maclean headed back to his castle at Bona, at the east end of Loch Ness, taking with him a dozen or more hostages – men, women and children.

When Lochiel returned home and found out about the bold raid he sent a band of caterans to capture two of Maclean's sons, who were out hunting in Glen Moriston. As soon as the news came that they had been caught, Lochiel put round the fiery cross to rally the clan. Within a few hours six or seven hundred Cameron warriors were ready, kitted out with weapons and food.

Hearing of their advance Hector sent word that, if they did not retreat, he would kill all the hostages. Lochiel replied that if any of the hostages were killed the same fate would overtake his sons. An offer of a prisoner exchange and a parley was sent by Lochiel, but Hector would have none of it. Proud and angry, he was surrounded and out-numbered by Lochiel's men, but was determined to die fighting.

One by one the hostages were killed and their bodies thrown over the battlements and Hector's sons were duly hanged before the castle walls in retaliation, as their father looked on. The Camerons then shot fire arrows into the castle, broke down the door and rushed the place, smashing it to pieces and killing madly once within.

Hector died fighting, as he had wished, but his death came at a cost to his people. The castle was never rebuilt, the memory of the murdered prisoners haunting the place. In the nineteenth century even the foundations were removed to help build the Caledonian Canal. To this day it is known as 'Castle Spirit'. One can visit the site, but few people do.

CHAPTER EIGHT

Pen and Paintbrush in the Highlands

THE HIGHLANDS, ITS PEOPLE and its animals have attracted numerous writers and artists over the years, and this was particularly the case in the nineteenth century – an era in which the area was 'discovered', and its people and customs often romanticised, by numerous literary and artistic greats.

Sir Walter Scott was one of the pivotal figures in this movement, and his historical novels did much to alter the British public's perception of Highland life. While he is best known for his books on characters such as Rob Roy, one of his earliest works was a short story about droving.

Entitled *The Two Drovers*, it was included in *Chronicles of the Canongate*, the first work of fiction to which the author put his own name. Published in 1827, the story is based on an account of a strange happening given to Scott's father. Whether the tale is historically accurate is not known but, as the author's grandfather was himself a drover, Scott is likely to have heard plenty of stories from the past. Either way, Sir Walter certainly knew something of the profession, as was reflected by his preface to the tale:

The Highlanders, in particular, are masters of this difficult trade of driving, which seems to suit them as well as the trade of war. It affords exercise for all their habits of patient endurance and active exertion. They are required to know perfectly the drove-roads, which lie over the wildest tracts of the country, and to avoid as much as possible the highways which distress the feet of the bullocks, and the turnpikes, which annoy the spirit of the drover; whereas, on the broad green or grey track, which leads across the pathless moor, the herd not only move at ease and without taxation, but, if they mind their business, may pick up a mouthful of food by the way. At night, the drovers usually sleep along with their cattle, let the weather be what it will; and many of these hardy men do not once rest under a roof during a journey on foot from Lochaber to Lincolnshire. They are paid very highly for the trust reposed is of the last importance, as it depends on their prudence, vigilance and honesty whether the cattle reach the final market in good order and afford a profit to the grazier. But as they maintain themselves at their own expense, they are especially economical in that particular. At the period we speak of, a Highland drover was victualled for his long and toilsome journey with a few handfuls of oatmeal and two or three onions, renewed from time to time, and a ram's horn filled with whisky, which he used regularly, but sparingly, every night and morning. His dirk or skene dhu (ie black knife) so worn as to be concealed beneath the arm, or by the folds of the plaid, was his only weapon, excepting the cudgel with which he directed the movements of the cattle. A Highlander was never so happy as on these occasions. There was a variety in the whole journey, which exercised the Celt's natural curiosity and love of motion; there were the constant change of place and scene, the petty adventures incidental to the traffic, and the intercourse with the various farmers, graziers and traders, intermingled with occasional merry-makings, not the less acceptable to Donald as they were void of expense; and there was the conscious-ness of superior skill; for the Highlander a child amongst flocks is a prince amongst herds, and his natural habits induce him to disdain the shepherd's slothful life, so that he feels himself nowhere more at home than when following a gallant drove of his cattle in the character of their guardian.

This insightful preface preceded the story itself – a tale that shows that, when out on the drove roads, matters sometimes reached an unlikely end.

The drovers in question – Robin Vig M'Combich (young Robin) and a young Englishman, Harry Wakefield – set off together from Doune, each with their own drove of cattle. Robin was small, light on his feet and very active; Harry, six feet tall, and full of life, was generally cheerful but occasionally prone to fight.

Before they left, Robin's aunt, who had the second sight, warned her nephew not to take his dirk with him, as she could envisage blood on his hands. Laughing this off, Robin gave the dirk to a friend, Hugh Morrison, who would be following with another drove.

Robin and Harry enjoyed each other's company, passing the time in singing, and the Scotsman taught his friend a word or two of Gaelic on the way. On reaching Cumberland they each sought overnight pasture for their respective cattle. Through a misunderstanding in their dealings with the local landowner, it turned out that Robin got a field of good grass for his drove, while Harry's herd were given much poorer ground.

After leaving their cattle in their allotted grazings the two drovers met up at the inn where they were to spend the night. Harry made some attempt to patch up the disagreement, but Robin would have none of it. Then Harry turned violent and went for his old companion with his fists, knocking him to the ground. Robin, who was not used to that kind of fighting and whose pride was badly hurt by the jeering of the English onlookers, rushed out to recover his dirk from Hugh Morrison. With revenge his all-powerful passion, he struck Harry in the heart with his blade.

Surrendering at once to a constable, Robin was taken to the prison at Carlisle. He was found guilty of murder and condemned to death. He accepted the verdict manfully, his

Highland pride avenged. And so the story of *The Two Drovers* ends.

Artists were equally attracted to the drovers and to cattle, especially in the Victorian era. Amongst the most famous was Edwin Landseer, who was born in London in 1802. He was twenty-two when he discovered the Highlands and was immediately enthralled by the scenery and the wildlife, particularly the deer. Landseer came to know the people and their way of life through painting them both at work and in their homes.

He soon found patrons aplenty among the former clan chiefs. These men, many of whom had since professed loyalty to the crown in exchange for dukedoms or other titles, were keen to promote their estates as sporting venues and reckoned Landseer's paintings, particularly of hunting, would move this process on.

Soon after his arrival in the north Landseer found his way, as so many artists did, to Abbotsford. There he painted Sir Walter Scott and his dogs repeatedly. He also painted a frontispiece and designs for the pages of the Waverley novels.

During this time Scott may have told him about droving, or might even had read him the story of *The Two Drovers*, so that he had some idea of what droving entailed. Either way, in 1835 he painted 'A Scene in the Grampians – the Drover's Departure'. It is a wonderful picture, full of relevant detail, and it tells a story of the closeness of family and community life in the Highlands.

In the painting a young man about to set off with his

drove embraces his child. An older man, the drover's father, knows the hazards of the journey and is a little sad and anxious for his son. His wife and daughter comfort him and his son's young wife pours a dram into a ram's horn for the road. Meanwhile a young couple, probably neighbours, are having a farewell talk.

In the distance others are gathering and the cattle, sheep and goats are beginning to make a move. The young boy watching the dogs and the puppy teasing the hen with her chicks shows the closeness, not only of the family members but also of the family's bond with their livestock. The hills in the distant haze give an idea of the length and wildness of the drover's journey ahead.

A friend of Landseer's, Thomas Sidney Cooper (1803–1902), while less well known, was an even more accomplished painter of cattle. Although born in humble circum stances in Canterbury, his painting eventually brought him great wealth. Cooper named one of his more famous paintings – of a large bull, with cow and calf – 'The Monarch of the Meadows' after Landseer's famous 'Monarch of the Glen.'

Both Landseer and Cooper were commissioned to do paintings for Queen Victoria. She and Prince Albert were very appreciative of their work.

Cooper depicted a Highland drover, resting beside a pony, with his faithful collie dog. It's good that the dog is remembered – as dogs were such an essential part of droving. Cooper delighted in painting Highland cattle in remote parts of the country, as did a growing number of other artists of the time. The Highlands were becoming a happy hunting ground for artists as well as for sportsmen. These powerful, yet surprisingly gentle, beasts with their auburn colouring and their upswept horns came to embody the Highlands for the Victorian artists. Soon no rural scene was complete without them.

One artist in particular, Louis Bosworth Hurt (1856–1929), became famous for his paintings of the Highlands and its cattle. Born in Derbyshire, he kept a small herd of Highland cattle of his own, so that they were readily available for accurate drawing and painting. He travelled widely in the Highlands, depicting the cattle in their natural environment – by lochs, being driven from the hills, while grazing and watering. One painting in particular, 'On Rannoch Moor', which depicts Highland cattle by a rushing burn and swathes of mist on the hills, is really magnificent. It is interesting to note that Hurt always included one dark-haired beast among a group of Highlanders. Perhaps he knew that Highland cattle were originally black.

Other painters – such as Richard Ansdell, Robert Watson, George Turner and Wright Barker – all showed Highland cattle at various stages of their journey from the hills to market. And one of their more interesting contemporaries was Joseph Denovan Adam (1841–1896), who lived in Stirling, where he ran a school of animal painting and kept live animals, including Highland cattle, for his students to paint. His highly-regarded work may be seen in Stirling's Smith Art Gallery and Museum.

Balmoral Castle, 1849
By Michel Bouquet © Aberdeen Art Gallery & Museums Collections

The work of all these artists was part of the cult of 'Balmorality' – the love of all things Highland, as was initiated in part by Queen Victoria and Prince Albert. The royals and their artistic followers certainly brought the area, until then largely unknown, to the attention of a fairly wide section of the public. They may also have helped to draw attention to the plight of many Highland people at the time. After all, the Crofters' Act, which gave crofters security in their holdings, was passed in 1886. The royals also encouraged the breeding of Highland cattle, which are now popular world-wide.

With the advent of the camera, Charles Reid's photographs of cattle came to the fore. Born in Aberdeenshire in 1837, by the 1880s he had become one of the most prominent animal photographers in Scotland, and gave lectures

Highlander family on way to hill pasture
By Charles Reid, courtesy of Jim Reid

on the subject to the Edinburgh Photographic Society. He died in 1929.

His son, also called Charles, was born in 1867 and carried on his father's business – taking pictures of rural scenes and all kinds of farm animals, which were often used in calendars. His grandson, Andrew Fraser Reid, continued the family tradition by taking photographs of cattle and heavy horses for farmers, Government agencies and so on. Many can be found in farmhouses today. Groups of Highland cattle, with calves and followers, in the hills, on ferries – all in black and white and attributable by the initials 'C.R.' in one corner – make attractive pictures. There is no posing here, the cattle are caught on the hoof. The three generations of Reids have left us a treasured store of 'actualities.'

Cattle swimming on drove
By Charles Reid, courtesy of Jim Reid

Cattle in hill grazing
By Charles Reid, courtesy of Jim Reid

In later times, as photographic processes became more and more sophisticated, many talented photographers working in the Highlands emerged. Robert Adam, Erskine Beveridge and MEM Donaldson, a lady of means, who trundled her equipment in a little trolley, all produced photographs of quality, but mainly of landscapes, buildings and people. Livestock did not feature so much in their work.

Margaret Fay Shaw, from South Uist, was another photographic pioneer, whose pictures act as excellent early recordings of life in the islands in the early 1900s. Today Colin Baxter, Laurie Campbell and others photograph wildlife and livestock, particularly Highland cattle. These are, of course, brilliantly photogenic and Baxter has them in calendars and posters which sell widely and well.

CHAPTER NINE

Today

AS THE NINETEENTH CENTURY progressed, farming methods were changing. Many of the 'improving' landowners were making their farms over to sheep; globalisation was on its way with the development of the colonies; the law of supply and demand was in fluctuating operation; and many estates were being managed largely for sport rather than agriculture. The small crofter with two or three cows and followers was on his way out, and the old kinship between humans and beasts was largely lost.

In the Highlands, resistance to foul weather – snow, gales, blizzards and salt spray – was always of the greatest importance in livestock. Highland cattle were perhaps the beasts most suited to the conditions, with their thick shaggy outer coats, their soft insulating undercoats and a fringe to shelter their eyes. They can be out-wintered, can calve in the snow, and can survive in peat bogs and on the poorest grazing. The cows are excellent mothers, docile unless threatened when with young, their milk is rich and the breed provides lean meat of the finest quality which is very much in demand.

In 1884 the first herd book of Highland cattle was published, thus making the breed one of the oldest to be

Cattle and snow, outwintered Highlanders
© Roy Dennis

registered. Highlanders are now found in many parts of the world – Canada, North America, Australia, New Zealand, Argentina and Peru. Lately, in the early twenty-first century, a number have been exported to Russia. It is hoped they can survive the country's harsh winters and that their horns may deter hungry wolves!

Even Glasgow City Council has its own fold of about 100 Highland cattle, which it keeps in Pollock Country Park. Each of the beasts is named in Gaelic and they can be seen grazing in the park. They go to shows all over the country and win numerous prizes.

Owing to their hardiness, Highlanders were also favoured as crosses with other breeds. In 1947 the Cadzow brothers bought the island of Luing, in Argyll. Here they established a herd of shorthorns crossed with Highlanders. This made for a hardy breed, called Luing cattle, which was recognised and registered in 1965 and which prospers in the Highlands and islands today.

In 1945 JW Hobbs came from Canada to establish the Great Glen Cattle ranch, based on his experience of ranching in North America. Working from his home at Inverlochy Castle he set about reclaiming a large area of derelict land between Spean Bridge and Fort William. The area was covered with bracken, heather, and large swathes of bog. Draining, ploughing, levelling, liming and fertilising were all undertaken and open sheds were erected to provide shelter for the beasts in the worst of the weather. They were to be out-wintered and fed silage made on the reclaimed arable land.

Hobbs, known as Joe, took an intense personal interest in his ranch and would ride on horseback with his 'cowboys' rounding up the cattle. Eventually he had 12,000 beasts on some 10,000 acres of land – a reflection of the poor nature of the soil, despite his considerable investments and improvements.

He and his wife were well liked and were associated with many good causes. In 1956 he was given the freedom of Fort William. However, in 1961, suffering from ill-health, Joe sold the ranch to a Mr Mackay from Ayrshire, who sold it on without the cattle. So ranching in Scotland is no more, but the cattle sheds can still be seen near the road to the Fort.

Today, now that we have got BSE out of the way, Scottish beef can recapture the fame it always had in Europe and the French can once again enjoy Highland 'rosbif'. Diseases such as BSE would have been unknown in older times, before the importing of unchecked feedstuffs and overcrowding in stuffy byres and milking parlours. Foot-and-mouth disease had always been treated by the application of Archangel tar. Later, checks for brucellosis were carried out regularly, as they are today. Tuberculosis is still monitored and now blue tongue is too.

In 1981 an interesting experiment was undertaken. John Keay, a traveller and writer, set out to fulfil an ambition he had had for many years – to take a drove of cattle from the islands to the market at Crieff. Undeterred by doubt and discouragement, he made careful plans, surveying the proposed route and assessing the possible dangers.

He had with him a vet, a climber, a stockman and his wife. They were to be accompanied by a television crew from the BBC.

The drove consisted of seventeen bullocks from Knoydart, thriteen more to follow and a cow from South Uist 'said to be in calf'. They soon developed a rapport with the drove, giving the 'boys' names. The cow, christened Matilda, led the others astray, but they came to love her too.

They reached the mainland from Skye at Kylerhea, the

cattle packed tight as sardines in an open rowing boat. The
SSPCA, who were keeping an eye on things, did not approve
of the traditional cattle 'swim'. From Glenelg they made
their way to Arnisdale, then on to Kinlochhourn and south.

They had their problems. One bullock developed
pneumonia and arthritis and had to be taken by trailer to
Broadford. At one point some of the animals suffered from
'floppy horns' – a strange affliction which was thankfully
cured by a change of cattle feed. Foot baths became essential
and were quite awkward to manage with the reluctant boys!

By the twelfth day they had covered sixty of the 200
miles to Crieff. They observed the Sabbath and found most
landowners and crofters helpful in providing night stances.
They took turns as watchers or sleepers in a tent. No heather
beds for them! After days of slog and danger negotiating
burns, peat hags, and bridges, there were occasions of
sheer delight – hill-top views, sunrises and sunsets, so well
described by Keay in his book, *Highland Drove*, as this
lyrical extract reflects:

> '*When the sinking sun threw a dazzling shaft
> straight at us the pile took fire, outlining each beast
> in a shaggy blur of flame. From feathered feet to
> bleached forelocks they blazed in glory. Their horns,
> honed and polished by the glare, were born aloft as
> trophies. Watching them was like seeing a vision. A
> crowd of birch saplings bowed beside the road. I
> swear there was music.*'

Reaching Crieff, they were welcomed by a police escort. Crowds lined the streets, clapping and even patting the beasts. Some experts had said that the big heavy cattle of today would not manage the walk as their hardy predecessors had. But here they were! The big day came and the boys fetched good prices. It was a sad parting. But Matilda duly gave birth – so all was not lost.

There are signs – small signs, but signs nevertheless – that cattle may be coming back to the status they so richly deserve in the economics of Highland agriculture.

Crofters on the Balmacara estate, near Kyle of Lochalsh, which is owned by the National Trust for Scotland, are being encouraged to revert to the old-fashioned ways of

Traditional methods of crofting at Drumbuie
Courtesy of the National Trust for Scotland

using land, under a Traditional Croft Management Scheme. Initiated in 2007, the project's objectives are 'to encourage and support the continuation and development of traditional, rotational cropping in the townships of Drumbuie, Duirnish and Plockton.' Further aims are: to encourage and support the retention of cattle within these crofting townships; to encourage the expansion of species-rich hay meadows and the preference of hay production over that of silage; and to ensure that such support and encouragement is delivered in an administratively efficient and flexible manner.

The overall goal of the scheme is to encourage the continuation of traditional crofting practices as a means of ensuring the protection and enhancement of the increasingly rare croft landscapes and associated species and habitats, as well as to maintain the strong cultural identity associated with crofting life.

Payment is made to the crofters involved in proportion to the crops grown and the cattle reared. It is hoped such a scheme will be successful and will be adopted in other areas. To visit the croft lands of Drumbuie with its crops, its cattle and its wild flowers is an inspiration and a delight.

It seems that things may be moving in a hopeful direction. Numbers of sheep are diminishing as the system of subsidies changes and the regulations regarding the animals' detention grow ever more restrictive. Red deer are being culled in greater numbers too, as the hills cannot support such a large population. When they venture near roads, seeking sustenance, deer create hazards for passing traffic.

Potatoes at Drumbuie
Courtesy of the National Trust for Scotland

The 'trophies of the chase' are no longer essential to bedeck the halls of shooting lodges. There are enough there already. The 'sport' of the deer hunt, costly as it is, is still being indulged in, mostly by wealthy Europeans. But can crawling towards your prey attended by a ghillie, who knows every inch of the ground, who hands you your gun and tells you exactly what to do, be called a sport? Should a beast be shot, the stalker will see to the carcass, congratulate you and put you on your way to the summer lodge, where a lavish picnic lunch will await.

If those Europeans sitting in their offices in Brussels or Luxembourg would come to visit the Highlands, to see the acres of rushes and bracken, and the little bright green patches where the shielings once were, they might have another think about where to put their subsidies and how to frame their directives. May greed be kept out of any reckoning and common sense and equilibrium prevail.

Cattle will keep the land in good heart. With their slow movement, their trampling of weed seeds, their consumption of coarse grasses and other herbage and, of course, their manuring, they create their own valuable and self-sustaining ecosystem.

The caterans are no more, but a generation of 'cowboys', riding four-wheel bikes, could replace the herdboys of older times. They could get to know their charges and their individual ways and even come to love them as their forebears did.

Even today a farmer is judged by the number of cattle he has, though his daughter's dowry may not be a small herd of cows but is more likely to be the money fetched by his prize heifer. Even a wise farmer has so much to learn from watching his cattle beasts. Salt licks are fine, but have you seen how the island cattle go to the shore to find the nutrients they need? Sheep in parts of Orkney feed entirely on the produce of the beach. Could the scientists devise feed-stuffs for the cattle from the masses of seaweeds that make such tasty and health-giving dishes for humans? And cattle have an uncanny sense of 'hefting', of finding their way to known places for shelter, or resting, or even giving birth.

Plastic and artificial fibres have replaced so many natural

Cattle on the west coast, looking towards Rum
© Roy Dennis

animal products. Those lovely horn spoons and combs and beakers are now only the prized possessions of the few or exhibits in museums. Cattle should never be relegated to icon status. They should be celebrated as the essential element in Highland life. They should have the honour accorded to the Burghead bulls and to the Portmahomack cow and calf – vital creatures whose effigies were carved lovingly in stone for the wonder of generations to come.

Bibliography

Bil, Albert, *The Shieling 1600–1840*, John Donald, Edinburgh, 1990

Bonser, KJ, *The Drovers*, Newton Abbot, 1972

Carmichael, Alexander, *Carmina Gadelica*, Floris Books, Edinburgh, 1992

Cochrane, UF, *Facts and Folklore on Highland Cattle*, Busdubh Publishing, 1996

Cregeen, Eric, 'Recollections of an Argyllshire Drover', *Scottish Studies*, vol 3 part 2, 1959

Dennis, Roy, 'The Importance of Traditional Cattle for Woodland Diversity in the Scottish Highlands'

Dictionary of Scottish Art and Architecture, Woodbridge, Suffolk, Antique Collectors Club, 1994

Fairweather, Barbara, *Highland Livestock and its Uses*, Glencoe Folk Museum, 1976

Fraser, Allan, *The Bull*, Osprey Publishing Ltd, Reading, 1972

Gibson, Rob, *Plaids and Bandanas*, Luath Press, Edinburgh, 2003

Grant, IF, *Highland Folkways*, Routledge & Kegan Paul, London, 1961

Haldane, ARB, *The Drove Roads of Scotland*, Birlinn, Edinburgh, 1997

Keay, John, *Highland Drove*, John Murray, London, 1984

Lightfoot, Rev John, *Flora Scotica*, London, 1777

MacDonald, Colin, *Croft and Ceilidh*, Edinburgh and London, 1947

MacDonald, Colin, *Life in the Highlands and Islands of Scotland*, Edinburgh, 1999

MacHardy, Stuart, *School of the Moon*, Birlinn, Edinburgh, 2004

Pursey, BF, *Highland Cattle*, published privately, 1999

Sambrauss, HH, *A Colour Atlas of Livestock Breeds*, Wolfe Publishing Ltd, 1992

Thomson, Francis, *The Lore and Literature of Scottish Beasts*, Molendinar Press, Glasgow, 1978

Toulson, Shirley, *The Drovers*, Shire Publications, 1980

Transactions of the Gaelic Society of Inverness

Transactions of the Inverness Scientific Society and Field Club

Chronology

c.8500 BC	Oldest human settlement in Scotland (so far discovered) in Cramond.
c.8000 BC	Aurochs, the wild ox, thought to arrive in Britain.
c.84 AD	Romans under Agricola defeat Caledonians under Calgacus at the battle of Mons Graupius in the Highlands.
121	Romans leave Scotland and begin building Hadrian's Wall.
563	Columba establishes the monastery at Iona.
1124	David I crowned king and introduces feudalism to Scotland.
1310	Robert the Bruce attacked by a wild bull when out hunting.
1454	Battle of Clachnaharry fought over stolen cattle between the Mackintoshes and the Munros.
1657	Last wild aurochs shot in Poland.
1746	Battle of Culloden – Bonnie Prince Charlie's Jacobite army is defeated and the demise of the clan system speeded up.
1762	Land reform tenure acts as a catalyst for the Clearances to begin in earnest.
1770	Falkirk takes over from Crieff as Scotland's main droving tryst.
1773	Johnson and Boswell tour the Highlands on horseback.
1792	The 'Year of the Sheep' – crofters in Easter Ross drove the recently introduced sheep from the grazing essential for their cattle.

1803   Dorothy Wordsworth's tour of the Highlands.

1824   Edwin Landseer first visits the Highlands.

1827   Sir Walter Scott publishes *The Two Drovers*.

1838   Queen Victoria's coronation.

1848   Victoria purchases her 'dear paradise in the Highlands' – Balmoral Estate.

1864   Alexander Carmichael, an excise officer, begins collecting songs, poems, stories and folklore in the Western Isles.

1867   Charles Reid begins photographing the Highlands.

1882   The Battle of the Braes. The women of the settlement at Braes on Skye defy and defeat policemen sent to evict them from their homes.

1884   The first herd book of Highland cattle is published.

           Queen Victoria publishes *More Leaves from the Journal of our Life in the Highlands*, a book which demonstrates the depth of her affection for the area.

1886   The Crofters' Act, which gave security of tenure to crofters as well as fixed, fair rents, passed.

1945   JW Hobbs sets up Great Glen Cattle Ranch.

1947   Heck brothers try to recreate aurochs, by crossing other breeds including Highland cattle.

1965   Luing cattle created by the Cadzow brothers.

1981   John Keay recreates a cattle drove from the Outer Isles to Crieff.

2009   Heck cattle, beasts akin to the aurochs, arrive in Britain.

Index

Luath Press Limited
committed to publishing well written books worth reading

LUATH PRESS takes its name from Robert Burns, whose little collie Luath (*Gael.*, swift or nimble) tripped up Jean Armour at a wedding and gave him the chance to speak to the woman who was to be his wife and the abiding love of his life. Burns called one of 'The Twa Dogs' Luath after Cuchullin's hunting dog in Ossian's *Fingal*. Luath Press was established in 1981 in the heart of Burns country, and is now based a few steps up the road from Burns' first lodgings on Edinburgh's Royal Mile.
Luath offers you distinctive writing with a hint of unexpected pleasures.

Most bookshops in the UK, the US, Canada, Australia, New Zealand and parts of Europe either carry our books in stock or can order them for you. To order direct from us, please send a £sterling cheque, postal order, international money order or your credit card details (number, address of cardholder and expiry date) to us at the address below. Please add post and packing as follows: UK – £1.00 per delivery address; overseas surface mail – £2.50 per delivery address; overseas air-mail – £3.50 for the first book to each delivery address, plus £1.00 for each additional book by airmail to the same address. If your order is a gift, we will happily enclose your card or message at no extra charge.

Luath Press Limited
543/2 Castlehill
The Royal Mile
Edinburgh EH1 2ND
Scotland
Telephone: 0131 225 4326 (24 hours)
Fax: 0131 225 4324
email: sales@luath.co.uk
Website: www.luath.co.uk